GREAT AMERICAN CAKES

Great American Cakes

LORRAINE BODGER

WARNER BOOKS

A Warner Communications Company

Copyright © 1987 by Lorraine Bodger and Jane Ross Associates, Inc.

All rights reserved.
Warner Books, Inc., 666 Fifth Avenue, New York, NY 10103

W A Warner Communications Company

Produced by Jane Ross Associates, Inc.

Printed in the United States of America
First Warner Trade paperback printing: November 1988
10 9 8 7 6 5 4 3 2 1

Library of Congress Cataloging in Publication Data
Bodger, Lorraine.
Great American Cakes.
1. Cake. 2. Cookery, American. I. Title.
TX771.B63 1987 641.8'653 87-6245
ISBN 0-446-38666-9 (pbk.) (U.S.A.)
0-446-38667-7 (pbk.) (Canada)

Book design and illustrations by Lorraine Bodger

Dedicated to my dear friends Jenny Snider and Joel Mason

Many thanks to the following skilled testers, discerning tasters,
generous contributors and helpful professionals:
Ruth Abrams; Lowell Bodger; Maggie Curran;
Delia Ephron and Jerome Kass; Stephen Javna;
Hiroko Kiiffner; Frances McLaughlin; Marnie Mueller;
Bill Rose; Jane Ross and Ed Brennan;
Blanche Small; Judy Stern; Candy Systra

Contents

Introduction 9

CHAPTER 1   Making Cakes 11

CHAPTER 2   Seven Basic Layer Cakes and How to Decorate Them 31

CHAPTER 3   Fabulous Chocolate Cakes 47

CHAPTER 4   Pound Cakes, Tea Loaves and Snack Cakes 61

CHAPTER 5   Yeast Coffeecakes and Quick Coffeecakes 71

CHAPTER 6   Cakes with Fresh Fruit 85

CHAPTER 7   Favorite Traditional Cakes 97

CHAPTER 8   Birthday Cakes and How to Decorate Them 111

CHAPTER 9   Extravagant Cakes for Special Occasions 125

CHAPTER 10   Christmas Cakes 143

CHAPTER 11   Frostings, Fillings and Glazes 161

Index 174

Introduction

I baked my first cake when I was six. My best friend Susie and her mother came over to our pink house in Tenafly, New Jersey, to spend a winter afternoon baking with me and my mother. We had plans to make a batch of little rolled-up coffeecakes, from my grandmother's famous recipe.

I was crazy about eating those cakes, but I found that I loved making them even more than eating them because it pleased my six-year-old heart tremendously to perform magic, to create something called dough out of what seemed to me an improbable combination of flour, sugar, butter, milk and eggs. Susie and I, standing on chairs to reach the kitchen counter, were allowed to roll out the dough, then gently spread butter and jam on it and sprinkle it ever so carefully with raisins and nuts. With a little discreet adult help, we rolled it up and cut it in pieces—and 25 long minutes later were rewarded with perfectly baked, perfectly delicious Quick Rich Little Coffeecakes.

The magic and the satisfaction of baking won me over right away, and that early experience of baking as a shared activity made a deep impression on me. I still love to bake with my friends whenever I can and the ideas for some of my best cakes have emerged from those happy afternoons. One summer, in a farm kitchen with the Catskill Mountains showing off outside the window, Candy and I folded fresh-picked raspberries into butter sponge cake batter—the genesis of the recipe for Raspberries-and-Cream Cake. And I baked with Patrick, in his city kitchen overlooking the Hudson River, inventing a wonderful Chocolate Grand Marnier Torte for a dinner party. My friend Delia and I experimented for years, trying to come up with the world's best coconut cake, and in her honor I finally buckled down and got it right; the final version, Fresh Coconut Layer Cake, was pronounced sensational.

Baking cakes with friends is intimate, punctuated with good talk and a certain amount of boisterousness, but testing recipes for a cookbook is serious business. You can't fool around and make mistakes. I did most of the recipe development and plenty of recipe testing alone in my kitchen, with the radio tuned to WNYC. Though solitary, it was an infinitely pleasant and comforting activity, soothing in its familiarity and orderliness. Cakes went into and came out of the oven in a constant stream and any lucky friend, neighbor or relative who passed through was presented with a package of whatever cake was being tested. My husband Lowell and I just couldn't (and wouldn't allow ourselves to) consume all that cake by ourselves, but I still regretted it the minute a cake walked out the door.

Cakes are such a part of my life that I often find myself identifying special occasions by the cakes I've made for them. I think of my friend Eleanor's seventieth birthday as an enormous two-tiered heart-shaped cake piped with a nosegay of pink and yellow spring flowers. My youngest brother's wedding was a glorious double-diamond-shaped cake frosted in peach-color buttercream and topped with fresh flowers. (There's a flip side, too: Many years ago I made a rainbow wedding cake for a dear friend, who now likes to say that her memory of the cake long outlasted the marriage.) I remember Jenny's forty-second birthday as one large and ten small strawberry shortcakes, and Joel's forty-third was a chocolate sponge roll filled with mocha buttercream and whipped cream, topped with chocolate sauce—transported from my house to his in a giant cardboard mailing tube.

My male friends invariably ask for chocolate cake with chocolate frosting when offered a choice on their birthdays. One happily married man I know swore he would follow me to the ends of the earth for my Light Chocolate Cake with Creamy Chocolate Frosting and Crisp Almond Macaroons. His wife wasn't too worried, but I appreciated the thought. My own husband, a purist, always requests Chocolate Pound Cake, with no vanilla glaze decoration to get between him and the chocolate, thank you very much.

I started my baking career standing on a chair to reach the linoleum kitchen counter. Nowadays I bake in an apartment kitchen not even half the size of that small suburban kitchen in Tenafly, and instead of the giant Mixmaster my mother used, I have one portable mixer, one full-size food processor and one compact food processor. Now the war about who gets to lick the spoon is fought with my husband instead of my two brothers. But the essential joy of baking hasn't changed one bit, and I've put a lifetime of that enjoyment into this book.

Lorraine Bodger

Making Cakes

FOLLOWING THE RECIPES
EQUIPMENT
INGREDIENTS
BASIC TECHNIQUES
BAKING THE CAKE
STORING THE CAKE
FILLING, FROSTING AND GLAZING
DECORATING PRIMER

Baking a cake from a recipe is not hard; you've probably done it many times. However, just as different bakers have their own ways of doing things, so different cookbooks have their own styles of presenting information and recipes. That's why it is important for you to read this chapter whether you are a novice or an experienced baker: Chapter 1 will get you started the right way, with explanations of ingredients, equipment, techniques and everything else you'll want to know to use this book efficiently and to be completely successful at baking cakes.

In addition to giving you basic baking information, Chapter 1 tells you how to fill and frost your cakes and offers an easy-to-use Decorating Primer with instructions for creating simple, delightful cake decorations.

FOLLOWING THE RECIPES

The recipe format in this book is simple and easy to follow; anything you don't understand is explained here in Chapter 1. The most important thing you must do is READ THE RECIPE ALL THE WAY THROUGH BEFORE YOU BEGIN.

GETTING STARTED

If you follow the first section of each recipe line by line, you'll arrive at step 1 with all systems go.

BAKING PAN: This line tells you what pan or pans you'll need; see EQUIPMENT (page 13) for more information about the shape of any required pan.

PAN PREPARATION: Tells you what to do to the pan before you put batter in it. There are three possibilities:

1. GREASE: Using a pastry brush or a piece of paper towel, apply a thin film of softened butter or margarine to the bottom and sides of the pan.

2. GREASE AND FLOUR: Grease as described above, add a spoonful or two of flour and tap the pan, tilting it in all directions so the flour coats the bottom and sides.

3. GREASE; LINE WITH WAXED PAPER; GREASE THE WAXED PAPER; DUST WITH FLOUR: Grease the pan as described above. Cut a piece of waxed paper to fit the bottom of the pan and press it in place in the greased pan. Apply a thin film of butter or margarine to the waxed paper and coat with flour as described above.

NOTE: To line a jelly roll pan with waxed paper, simply tear off a piece of waxed paper several inches longer than the pan, center the paper over the pan, press it smoothly onto the bottom and sides of the pan and fold the excess over the ends.

PREHEAT OVEN: Tells you to put your oven thermometer in the center of the middle rack of the oven and set the oven to the required temperature at least 15 minutes before baking a cake. If the thermometer indicates an incorrect setting, adjust the oven control and wait until the temperature is correct.

BAKING TIME: Tells you how long the cake must stay in the oven. If a range of times is given, for example "25–30 minutes," test for doneness after 25 minutes but leave the cake in the oven for up to 30 minutes if necessary. (More on baking and testing for doneness on pages 20–21.)

INGREDIENTS: The list of ingredients tells you everything you will need for making the cake, including frosting and decorations. Make no substitutions, except for optional ingredients, fillings and frostings.

Assemble the ingredients, carrying out any short instructions mentioned in the list. For instance, "2 eggs, beaten" means: Put the eggs in a small bowl and beat them now, so that they are ready when you need them. A few ingredients, like cocoa powder or confectioners' sugar, will require sifting—this will be noted in the list of ingredients. (Flour is rarely sifted for these recipes; there is absolutely no need to sift it unless specifically stated.)

Most recipes require "butter, softened," so take the correct amount of butter out of the refrigerator an hour before you'll need it. (You can cut the butter into pats so it softens faster, or mash it with a fork to soften it.)

RECIPE STEPS

It is important to follow all the recipe steps carefully. If you have questions, refer to BASIC TECHNIQUES, pages 18–20.

NOTE: As you add, mix, beat and blend the ingredients, be sure to scrape down the sides of the bowl quite often with a rubber spatula.

EQUIPMENT

You probably already have most of the equipment required for cake-baking—bowls, spoons, baking pans, rubber and metal spatulas and so on. Special equipment for cake-decorating is described in the DECORATING PRIMER, pages 25–30.

BAKING PANS: Use shiny, heavy aluminum pans (not dark or glass ones) of the size specified in the recipe.

CAKE BOARDS: Disposable cardboard circles and rectangles in a variety of sizes; perfect for transporting and giving away your cakes or when you don't have a large enough serving platter. Not essential but a great convenience. Available in cake-decorating stores and kitchenware departments.

CAKE TESTERS: Wooden toothpicks are adequate but 6-inch wooden skewers are better; do not use metal skewers.

DOUBLE BOILER: Two saucepans that fit together, one above the other, with a tight-fitting lid.

ELECTRIC MIXER: Use either a portable, three-speed mixer with a strong motor or a stand mixer.

pastry blender

pastry cutter

wire whisks

FOOD PROCESSOR (FULL-SIZE OR COMPACT): Not an essential, but efficient for chopping and grinding nuts, cutting butter into dry ingredients and a few other cake-baking tasks.

GRATER: A four-sided metal grater is the most useful for these recipes. Some people like a hand-held rotary grater for grinding nuts, but I prefer a food processor.

MEASURING CUPS: For liquids, use clear glass or plastic one-cup measures with distinct markings and good pouring spouts; for dry ingredients, use a set of graduated measures (¼ cup, ⅓ cup, ½ cup and one cup) with flat rims.

MEASURING SPOONS: Have at least one set in graduated sizes— ¼ teaspoon, ½ teaspoon, one teaspoon and one tablespoon.

PASTRY BLENDER: Used for cutting butter into dry ingredients. Buy a good-quality one with a wooden handle and sturdy wires.

PASTRY BRUSHES (½-INCH AND ONE-INCH WIDTHS): For spreading butter on cake pans, hot glaze on cake layers, icing on miniature cakes. They suffer a lot of wear and tear, so buy high-quality brushes and keep them scrupulously clean with hot water and soap.

PASTRY CUTTER: Useful for cutting the dough for coffeecakes and small pastries.

SPATULAS: Rubber spatulas are used for scraping down the mixing bowl and for folding; metal spatulas are used for loosening certain cakes from their pans and for spreading fillings and frostings.

STRAINERS: Use a small fine-mesh strainer for sifting small amounts of dry ingredients or for straining fresh lemon juice. A larger fine-mesh strainer is excellent for sifting flour or confectioners' sugar.

THERMOMETERS: An *oven thermometer (mercury type)* is a necessity. Put it in the center of the oven when you preheat, to be sure the oven is reaching the correct temperature. (If your oven is consistently off by more than 25 degrees, have it adjusted by a professional.)

An *instant-reading thermometer* is needed for testing the temperature of the water mixed with yeast when making raised dough. A *candy thermometer* measures the temperature of boiling sugar syrup used in making certain frostings.

TIMER: There are many kinds; be sure yours is accurate and always set it when you put a cake in the oven.

WIRE RACKS (CAKE RACKS): Used for cooling the cakes. The best kind have wires that either criss-cross or are quite close together and have wire feet at least half an inch high to allow plenty of space for air to circulate below a cooling cake.

WIRE WHISKS: Have a small one for beating eggs and a medium-size one for mixing dry ingredients together.

INGREDIENTS

The following alphabetical list includes information on the ingredients you need for making the cakes in this book.

BAKING POWDER: Use double-acting baking powder and be sure it is fresh—buy a new can every few months.

BAKING SODA: Tends to form lumps in the box, so sift or crumble it before measuring.

BROWN SUGAR: The recipe will specify light or dark brown sugar. Use fresh, moist brown sugar and pack it firmly into the measuring cup. Break up any lumps before you add it to the other ingredients.

BUTTER: This means sticks of unsalted butter—not lightly salted, not whipped.

CAKE FLOUR: Cake flour is different from all-purpose flour and self-rising flour (*never* use self-rising flour for these recipes). Cake flour produces a more tender, delicate texture than all-purpose flour and is therefore more appropriate for some cakes. Use it when it is called for.

CHOCOLATE (GENERAL INFORMATION): You do not need fancy brands of chocolate for the recipes in this book, but you must use the real stuff—not chocolate-flavored substitutes. Buy reliable, clearly-labeled brands like Baker's, Nestlé and Hershey's.

Melt chocolate in a heavy saucepan over very low heat, stirring it constantly and watching it like a hawk to be sure it does not burn. Another method is to put the chocolate in an ovenproof bowl and let it melt in the oven at low heat.

Chocolate is often melted with butter or a liquid; however, when melting chocolate by itself, do not let even a drop of liquid get into it or it will stiffen.

Unsweetened chocolate: Generally available in convenient one-ounce squares; used only for cooking.

Semisweet chocolate: Also found in one-ounce squares; used mostly for cooking, but fine when grated or chopped for cake decoration.

Chocolate chips: Used strictly as decoration or stirred whole into batter, never melted as a substitute for semisweet chocolate.

White chocolate: Not really chocolate, but wonderful as decoration or chopped and stirred into frosting.

COCONUT: Most of us can't find time to grate fresh coconut meat (unless it's for Fresh Coconut Layer Cake, page 108), so packaged, sweetened, shredded or flaked coconut must usually suffice. Unsweetened, flaked coconut is available in bulk in many health food stores.

To remove the sweetening from packaged coconut: Rinse the coconut for a minute or two in a strainer under running water, stirring it around. Squeeze out the water. Spread the wet coconut on a jelly roll pan and leave it in a preheated 350° oven for 10–13 minutes, stirring several times. Take it out of the oven and let it cool. At this point it will not be toasted, just dried.

To toast unsweetened or sweetened coconut: Spread it on a jelly roll pan and leave it in a 350° oven for 5–10 minutes, stirring several times, until it turns pale golden brown. Remove it and let it cool.

CONFECTIONERS' SUGAR: Used for glazes and frostings. Measure by spooning lightly into a measuring cup and leveling off the top.

If a recipe calls for "1 cup confectioners' sugar, sifted," measure out a cup of the sugar and *then* sift it. If the recipe calls for "1 cup sifted confectioners' sugar," first sift some confectioners' sugar into a bowl and *then* measure out a cup of it.

CORN SYRUP: The recipe will specify light or dark.

DRIED FRUITS: This includes prunes, apricots, figs, currants, dates and others (see *Raisins*, below). Never use old, hard dried fruit in baking—it won't soften up in the baking process. Restore hard fruit to softness by soaking it briefly in hot or boiling water just until tender. Drain, pat dry on paper towels and then let it air-dry completely.

EGGS: Use fresh eggs graded *large*. Cold eggs are easiest to separate, but bring yolks, whites or whole eggs to room temperature before beating because they will achieve greater volume.

FLOUR: This means all-purpose flour. Don't sift all-purpose flour unless the recipe specifically calls for it; simply spoon it lightly into a measuring cup and level it off. Never tap, shake or pack the measuring cup.

GRATED LEMON OR ORANGE RIND: Use the larger punched holes of a four-sided grater to grate just the colored outer layer of a cold lemon or orange; do not grate the bitter white pith just below. Get all the little bits of rind out of the grater by brushing in and around the holes with a stiff pastry brush.

HEAVY CREAM: Sometimes called whipping cream. Keep it very cold for whipping and taste a drop or two before using it to be sure it is perfectly fresh.

Dried lemon or orange rind is not an acceptable substitute for freshly grated rind.

MILK: Use whole milk in these recipes.

NUTS: Nuts must be fresh or your cake won't be worth eating. Buy them packaged (although that is not a guarantee of freshness) or in bulk from a market with rapid turnover. Store the nuts in the freezer, refrigerator or another cool place and taste them before you use them. The flavor of stale or moldy nuts cannot be concealed, even in a baked cake.

Almonds: Don't blanch or toast almonds unless the recipe specifically calls for it. To blanch, put almonds in a pot of boiling water for a minute or so, drain and rinse well in cold water. Pinch the brown skins off. Dry first with paper towels and then on a jelly roll pan in a 300° oven for a few minutes, just until the almonds are crisp but not toasted.

To toast, spread blanched or unblanched almonds on a jelly roll pan and put them in a preheated 350° oven for 7–12 minutes, watching them carefully. Test for crispness by eating a *cooled* nut.

Hazelnuts (filberts): To toast, spread on a jelly roll pan and leave in a preheated 350° oven for 7–12 minutes, watching them carefully. Test by eating a *cooled* nut. Remove the papery, brown skins (as much as will come off) by rubbing a few hazelnuts at a time between your palms or in a rough dish towel.

Walnuts and pecans: For extra crispness, toast on a jelly roll pan for a few minutes in a 350° oven.

NOTE: *Chop* nuts in a food processor or nut chopper, or by hand in a wooden bowl; the chopped pieces should all be about the same size. *Grind* nuts in a food processor or rotary grinder; be careful not to turn the nuts to paste.

RAISINS: Use soft, plump seedless raisins, dark or light as called for in the recipe. Soak hard raisins in very hot water for 15–20 minutes to soften them.

SUGAR: This means granulated white sugar.

SUPERFINE SUGAR: Also called dessert sugar or bar sugar, this is a very finely granulated version of regular white sugar. It is extremely useful in cakes and frostings but sometimes a little difficult to find, so stock up on it when you see it. Do not try to make superfine sugar yourself.

UNSWEETENED COCOA POWDER: This means real cocoa powder (like Hershey's or Droste's), *not* the prepared, sweetened drink mixes.

VANILLA AND OTHER EXTRACTS: Use pure vanilla and almond extracts—no imitations allowed, with the exception of imitation coconut extract.

YEAST: The recipes in this book were tested with dry yeast granules, which are sold in ¼-ounce packets or in bulk (one packet equals a scant tablespoon of bulk dry yeast). Instructions for dissolving and using yeast are included in the recipes.

BASIC TECHNIQUES

ADDING DRY INGREDIENTS ALTERNATELY WITH LIQUID, IN THREE PARTS EACH, BEATING WELL AFTER EACH ADDITION: This is simply a gradual mixing process that produces properly blended batter with enough air beaten in to promote rising when the cake is baked.

BEATING: Means to mix ingredients rapidly to produce a smooth, amalgamated mixture. Beating also incorporates air, which is important in cake batters, fluffy egg whites and meringues, whipped cream, etc. I strongly recommend using an electric mixer.

BEATING EGG WHITES UNTIL THEY STAND IN FIRM, GLOSSY, MOIST PEAKS: First beat the whites at low speed until they are foamy. Switch up to medium speed and watch closely as the whites thicken enough to form soft, droopy peaks. Keep beating at medium speed *just* until whites hold stiff peaks that droop only a bit at the top. The peaks should still be moist and glossy-looking. Do not beat any further. (Overbeaten egg whites look dry and break up into clumps that slide around on a puddle of thin liquid.)

BLENDING: Means to mix the ingredients together, either with a spoon or an electric mixer, until smoothly and evenly combined.

CREAMING UNTIL LIGHT: To cream butter, beat until it is pale in color, smooth and light in texture—almost airy.

To cream butter and sugar until light, beat until the mixture is pale in color, well blended and as light and smooth as possible; if there is a high proportion of sugar to butter, the mixture will not be perfectly smooth.

CUTTING BUTTER INTO DRY INGREDIENTS: Add pats of cold butter to the bowl of dry ingredients and use a pastry blender to cut through the butter and mix it into the dry ingredients. Keep working until the butter is reduced to small bits and is evenly distributed. The mixture should look like crumbs or cornmeal.

This may also be done in a food processor, with the steel chopping blade and just a few bursts of power.

FOLDING: To incorporate one ingredient into another with a gentle but firm scooping and lifting motion, using a rubber spatula.

KNEADING: Yeast dough is mixed and brought to the proper consistency by this push-fold-turn sequence.

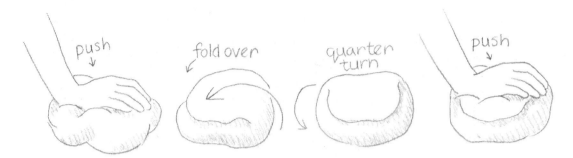

LINING ROUND PANS WITH WAXED PAPER CIRCLES: Put a cake pan on a piece of waxed paper and outline with a pencil. Stack the paper with one or two more pieces of waxed paper (as needed) and fold in half, matching up the edges of the outline. Fold in quarters, matching the edges again. Cut through all the layers of paper just inside the outline. Unfold and flatten.

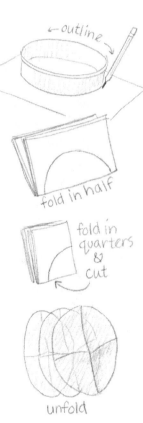

Grease a round pan. Center a waxed paper circle on the bottom of the pan and smooth it down. Grease the waxed paper circle.

MEASURING BUTTER: Each quarter-pound stick of butter equals eight tablespoons, so you can easily mark and cut off the amount you need even if the package has no tablespoon indications.

MEASURING DRY INGREDIENTS: Use a set of graduated measuring cups with flat rims (see EQUIPMENT, page 14). White sugar is spooned or scooped into a measuring cup and the cup leveled with a knife or narrow metal spatula. Brown sugar must be packed firmly into a measuring cup before leveling. Flour is spooned lightly into a measuring cup and then leveled with a knife or metal spatula; never tap or shake the measuring cup to level the flour.

Small amounts of baking powder, baking soda, cocoa powder, spices and other dry ingredients are measured in graduated measuring spoons and leveled with a knife or metal spatula.

MEASURING LIQUID INGREDIENTS: Use a clear glass or plastic measuring cup with distinct markings and a pouring spout (see EQUIPMENT, page 14). Put the cup on a flat surface, *bend down* so your eye is at cup level and fill the cup to the correct mark.

PUNCHING DOWN: After yeast dough has risen, it is turned out of the bowl onto a flat surface and deflated by punching it all over with your fist.

SIFTING: I use fine-mesh strainers for all sifting—small ones for small amounts of cocoa, etc., and larger ones for confectioners' sugar, flour and mixtures of dry ingredients. Simply spoon in the dry ingredients and tap the strainer (or stir with a spoon) over a bowl.

SPLITTING A LAYER IN HALF: If possible, put the layer in the freezer for an hour to firm. With a long, sharp knife, make shallow horizontal cuts around the perimeter of the layer, dividing it in half. Using these cuts as guides, carefully slice straight across the layer or in an arc.

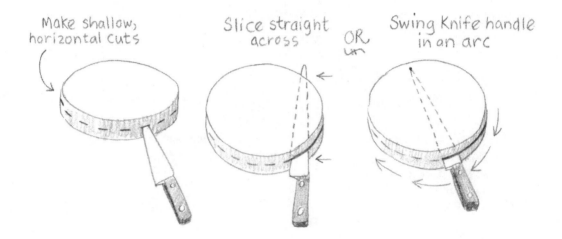

Make shallow, horizontal cuts

Slice straight across OR

Swing knife handle in an arc

BAKING THE CAKE

If you have followed the recipe instructions, your oven is preheated to the correct temperature, ready to receive the filled cake pans.

PLACING THE CAKE PANS IN THE OVEN: Pans are placed on the middle rack of the oven, with space between pans *and* space between the pans and the walls of the oven. If necessary, distribute the pans on the *two* middle racks, staggering the arrangement so that heat circulates freely, with one pan on the lower rack and two on the upper.

Do not open the oven while the cake is baking (until the last five to ten minutes of baking—see below); a sudden rush of cool air can make the cake fall.

TESTING FOR DONENESS: Toward the end of the baking period, begin to test for doneness. If the recipe gives one specific baking time (for instance, 30 minutes), begin testing five to ten minutes before the time is up. If the recipe gives a range of times (for instance, 25–30 minutes), begin testing after the shorter time has elapsed.

Test by inserting a wooden toothpick or wooden skewer in the center of the cake or, in the case of a tube cake, midway between the inner and outer walls of the cake pan. Withdraw the pick or skewer. If it comes out clean, with no batter or crumbs stuck to it, the cake is properly baked. If it has thick, damp batter clinging to it, the cake needs about ten more minutes of baking; if it has sticky crumbs on it, three to five more minutes will be enough. Test again after the additional baking. If the pick or skewer comes out clean and dry, remove the cake immediately.

Other signs of doneness: The top of the cake looks dry; the cake is pulling away from the sides of the pan; the cake springs back (slowly) after you press it lightly in the center.

COOLING THE CAKE: Most cakes are cooled *in the pan* on a wire rack (see EQUIPMENT, page 14) for ten minutes and then turned out of the pan to finish cooling right side up on the rack. Here's how to turn out the cake:

● Run a sharp knife around the cake to be sure it is not stuck to the pan.

● Cover the pan with an inverted wire rack. Flip the cake and rack and the cake will drop out of the pan onto the rack. Remove the pan. The cake is now wrong side up.

● Cover the cake with an inverted wire rack and flip again. Remove the top rack. The cake is now right side up.

Let the cake finish cooling on the rack.

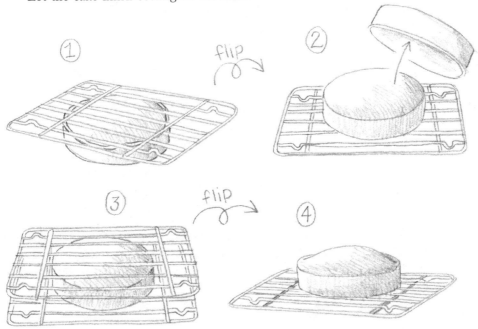

STORING THE CAKE

Cakes must be completely cool before you store them. Follow these guidelines for successful storage.

UNFROSTED LAYERS: To keep for several days at room temperature, wrap snugly in one or two layers of plastic and a layer of aluminum foil. For longer storage: Wrap as described, label and date the cake and store it in the freezer. Defrost in the refrigerator overnight or at room temperature for several hours.

POUND CAKES, FRUITCAKES AND OTHER CAKES WITH DENSE TEXTURES: These cakes will stay fresh for several days or more if you wrap them well in plastic or store in a cake preserver. To freeze: Wrap snugly in plastic and then aluminum foil. Defrost in the refrigerator overnight or at room temperature for several hours.

CUPCAKES, SMALL PASTRIES AND SINGLE SERVINGS OF SNACK CAKE: Wrap individually in plastic—they'll stay fresher. Freeze in plastic bags, six to eight per bag. Put an individually wrapped frozen cake or pastry in a brown bag lunch in the morning and by noon it will be ready to eat.

COFFEECAKES: Wrap snugly in plastic and eat as soon as possible because homemade coffeecake goes stale quickly. (Slightly stale coffeecake is vastly improved by gentle warming in the oven at low heat.) The best solution to the problem of staleness is to freeze whatever isn't eaten on the first day: Wrap snugly in plastic and then in aluminum foil. Label and date the package and freeze until needed.

Defrost in the refrigerator overnight, at room temperature for several hours or in a slow oven until thoroughly warmed.

CHEESECAKE: Store in the refrigerator, covered snugly, and bring to room temperature before serving. To freeze: Chill uncovered in the freezer until firm, then wrap well and return to the freezer.

CAKES FROSTED WITH BUTTERCREAM: Store in a cake preserver (or on a cake plate covered with a large inverted bowl) for up to a few hours; refrigerate for longer storage. Serve at room temperature. To freeze: Chill uncovered in the freezer until firm, then wrap well and return to the freezer. Defrost *unwrapped* in the refrigerator overnight or at room temperature for several hours.

CAKES FROSTED WITH SNOWDRIFT FROSTING (PAGE 166) OR OTHER EGG WHITE FROSTINGS: Do not refrigerate or freeze because the frosting will separate and fall apart. Store in a cake preserver and eat as soon as possible.

CAKES FILLED AND/OR FROSTED WITH PASTRY CREAM OR WHIPPED CREAM: Perishable fillings and frostings like these *must* be refrigerated. To freeze cakes with whipped cream frosting: Chill uncovered in the freezer until firm, then wrap well and return to the freezer. Defrost *unwrapped* in the refrigerator overnight or at room temperature for a few hours.

FILLING, FROSTING AND GLAZING

Filling goes between the layers of a layer cake; frosting goes on the top and/or sides of a cake; glaze is a thin icing, usually for the top of a cake.

ABOUT FILLINGS: The frosting you choose for the top of the cake can, of course, be used for the filling, too. Or the filling can be something quite different—chocolate pastry cream filling with vanilla buttercream frosting, for example. Just be sure to combine filling, frosting and cake that complement one another.

In Chapter 11 you will find a variety of flavored whipped creams and pastry creams perfect for fillings. Another rich, delicious alternative is to fold some unsweetened whipped cream into any flavor of pastry cream to make "pastry cream lightened with whipped cream." (This can be used for frosting as well as filling.)

Add interest to plain fillings by spreading cake layers with marmalade, apricot (or other) jam, jelly or fruit butter before spreading with filling. Or brush layers with rum, brandy or your favorite liqueur and then spread with filling. Give crunch to the filling by sprinkling it with chopped nuts, chopped chocolate or toasted coconut.

ABOUT FROSTINGS: Follow the frosting suggestions given with each recipe or make your own choice from Chapter 11 (pages 161–173). Use frosting generously and spread it only on completely cooled cakes.

ABOUT GLAZES: Glaze is used as garnish on rich but plain cake, on coffeecake and small yeast pastries and on top of frosting as a decoration. Glazes can be spread, poured or drizzled on cool or warm cakes; the glaze itself may be used warm or cool, depending on the recipe.

TINTING OR COLORING DECORATING FROSTING (PAGE 30) OR ANY OTHER WHITE FROSTING: For tinting (making pastel colors), add liquid food coloring a drop or two at a time to the bowl of frosting and stir briskly to distribute the color evenly.

For coloring (making bright or intense colors), use paste food coloring. Scoop up a bit of paste color on the tip of a toothpick and swirl it into the bowl of frosting. Stir briskly to distribute the color evenly. If desired, add more coloring a little at a time, keeping in mind that paste coloring is very concentrated.

AMOUNTS OF FILLING AND FROSTING: For a two- or three-layer cake, eight or nine inches in diameter, you need ¾–1 cup of filling between layers and 1½–2 cups of frosting for the top and sides. The amounts may vary according to the type of cake and the type of frosting (for instance, Snowdrift Frosting, page 166, should be applied more generously).

PROTECTING THE PLATTER: When you are filling, frosting, glazing or decorating any cake, protect the serving platter from drips and spills by tucking six-inch-wide waxed paper strips under the cake. With your fingers or a metal spatula, lift the edge of the cake and tuck a strip under it; work around the cake, tucking enough waxed paper strips under it to protect the platter completely.

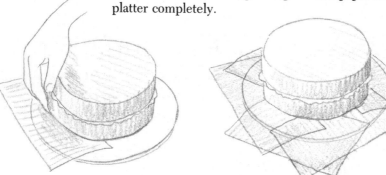

FILLING AND FROSTING A THREE-LAYER CAKE: First, level each layer by carefully slicing off any high spots with a sharp knife; proceed cautiously so you don't remove too much. Brush away any crumbs. (This step is easier if the layers are firmed in the freezer for an hour first.)

Center one layer wrong side up on a serving platter or cake board. Tuck waxed paper strips under the cake to protect the platter and spread the layer with ¾–1 cup of filling. Place the second layer wrong side up on the first layer. Spread ¾–1 cup of filling on it.

Place the third layer wrong side up on the second layer. Put 1½–2 cups of frosting on the top and spread from the center out to the edges. Spread some of the frosting from the top onto the sides, evening and smoothing the frosting to a uniform thickness. Smooth the frosting with a spatula dipped in hot water.

DECORATING PRIMER

This is a collection of quick and easy methods for making your frosted cakes prettier. There are two categories of decorations, each with a variety of possibilities which you may use one at a time or combine in any way you like:

● Super-easy, no-piping edible decorations applied to the frosting on the top and/or sides of the cake

● Simple piped decorations made with a standard pastry bag and tips, using regular frosting, Decorating Frosting (recipe follows on page 30) or whipped cream

SUPER-EASY, NO-PIPING, EDIBLE DECORATIONS

Here is a list of decorations that can be sprinkled, pressed or arranged on the top and/or sides of a frosted cake. Choose a design from the drawings below (and in the rest of the book) or invent your own design and carry it out according to the guidelines that follow the list.

NOTE: Starred items are suitable for pressing onto the sides of the cake, as described below (*Decorating the sides of the cake*).

- ● Dollops of whipped cream or pastry cream
- ★ Candies: Nonpareils, Jordan almonds, chocolate raisins or peanuts, chocolate coffee beans, jelly fruit slices, etc.
- ● Marzipan fruit
- ● Crystallized violets and other flowers
- ★ Colored sugars, dots and sprinkles
- ★ Chocolate sprinkles and chocolate chips
- ● Grated or chopped semisweet or white chocolate
- ★ Cookie crumbs
- ★ Chopped, slivered or sliced nuts
- ● Whole almonds, pistachios, hazelnuts or macadamias; walnut or pecan halves
- ● Candied ginger, glacé cherries and oranges
- ● Fruit: Grapes, strawberries and other berries, sliced bananas, canned pineapple, orange or lemon slices
- ● Dried fruit: Raisins, currants, apricot slivers or bits, sliced dates, etc.
- ● Slivers of orange or lemon peel: To make slivers, peel the lemon or orange thinly with a vegetable peeler. Cut the long strips into slivers with scissors.
- ★ Toasted or untoasted coconut

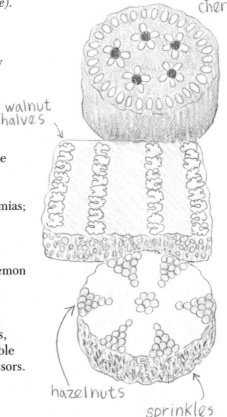

whole almonds & glacé cherries

walnut halves

hazelnuts

sprinkles

strawberry, pineapple slice, banana slices

lemon slivers

orange slices

tea roses

blueberry green grape

crystallized violets

ANCHORING THE DECORATIONS: Push each decoration into the frosting so it is firmly embedded (but not buried). When scattering small decorations like chips, sprinkles or chopped nuts on the top of the cake, be sure the frosting is still tacky enough to hold them. If it is not, first roughen the surface with a spatula.

DECORATING THE SIDES OF THE CAKE: To coat the sides of a frosted cake with chopped nuts, take some nuts in the cupped palm of your hand and press them into the frosting. Repeat until the sides are covered as thickly as you like.

MAKING GLAZE DESIGNS: Use a glaze that contrasts with the frosting—chocolate glaze on vanilla buttercream, vanilla glaze on chocolate frosting. Spoon the glaze into a heavy plastic bag and squeeze it down toward one corner of the bag. Twist the bag and seal with a twist-tie. Snip a tiny bit off the corner and squeeze out the glaze in a lattice pattern, a spiral, loops, etc. If you like, practice on a piece of waxed paper or an inverted cake pan before making the glaze design on the actual frosted cake.

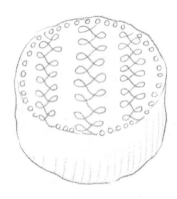

SIMPLE PIPED DECORATIONS

Piping is easy and fun when you keep it simple, avoiding complicated techniques or designs that require excessive planning, fancy flowers and overdone borders.

In addition to frosting, you will need decorating bags (sometimes called pastry bags), couplers and tips (sometimes called tubes).

FROSTING: Many of the frostings in Chapter 11 work well for simple piping; sweetened or flavored whipped cream (page 168) is also excellent. For the simple piping shown on the next few pages, you may want to use Decorating Frosting (recipe follows on page 30), which is a perfect piping consistency and can be tinted or colored as you like. (Do *not* use Decorating Frosting as a filling or frosting for a cake.)

DECORATING BAGS (PASTRY BAGS): You can buy reusable ones made of heavy plastic or plastic-lined muslin, but I prefer disposable, thinner plastic ones that come in packages of 24 and are very reasonably priced. Whichever style you choose, have several.

COUPLERS: Each coupler consists of a nozzle and a threaded ring for connecting the tip to the decorating bag. The coupler allows you to change tips quickly and easily, without filling a new decorating bag. You will need several.

TIPS (TUBES): These are the metal cones through which frosting is squeezed; they come in many standard shapes and sizes. For simple piping, buy plain round tips for writing and making looped shapes (#3, #5 and #7 are good choices), a few closed star tips for flowers and borders (#27, #30, #33 and #34), one or two open star tips for flowers and borders (#20 and #22) and one large star tip (#2D) for piping whipped cream rosettes.

GETTING STARTED: Begin by joining a decorating bag, coupler and round tip, following the manufacturer's instructions included with the coupler.

FILLING THE DECORATING BAG: Fold the bag down over your hand to form a wide cuff, as shown in the drawing. Use a metal spatula to fill the bag *half full*. Unfold the cuff, fold the sides in and roll the end down *or* simply twist the bag closed right above the frosting and hold it securely—use whichever technique is easiest for you. Holding the end closed, squeeze the bag to push out any trapped air.

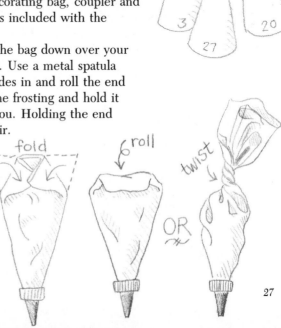

PRACTICING SIMPLE PIPING: Hold the folded or twisted end with one hand; with your other hand you will squeeze out the frosting in a smooth flow and guide the tip at the same time. Begin practicing on a piece of waxed paper.

Try a few straight lines: Hold the bag at about a 30–degree angle to the paper. Squeeze out the frosting smoothly and steadily with one hand while you move your other hand to make the line. The tip should just barely touch the surface of the paper without digging in or dragging. Practice until you feel comfortable.

Now try some dots: Hold the bag perpendicular to the paper with the tip just touching the surface. Squeeze out a little frosting. When the frosting forms a tiny mound, stop squeezing, lift up and move the tip away in a smooth motion. Make a whole row of dots.

When you are feeling comfortable with dots and lines, try some loops, scallops and curlicues and then some simple letters and numbers.

Unscrew the coupler, remove the round tip and attach a closed star tip. Practice straight lines, wavy lines and scallops. Next, use the dot technique described above to make a row of separate little flowers and then a row of flowers just touching each other—a flower border.

Spend some time experimenting with each different tip, making borders and criss-cross lines, flowers and wreaths, bows and faces.

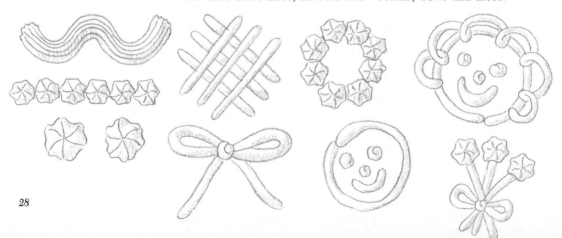

USING SIMPLE PIPING ON CAKES: There are many ways to enhance your cakes with simple borders, patterns of dots or flowers, criss-crossed lines, writing and so on. The drawings below will give you a few ideas; try your own designs, too. You may find it helpful to use a toothpick or wooden skewer to mark the design on the frosted cake before you start piping.

DECORATING FROSTING

MAKES ABOUT TWO CUPS

This recipe may be doubled or even tripled. The frosting does not need to be refrigerated, so you can make it ahead of time and begin decorating when you're ready, without having to wait for it to soften. Use Decorating Frosting *only* for piping.

½ cup solid white vegetable shortening
¼ cup (½ stick) butter, softened

1 teaspoon vanilla extract
3 cups sifted confectioners' sugar
Food coloring (optional)

In a large bowl, beat the vegetable shortening, butter and vanilla until light and smooth. Gradually add the confectioners' sugar, beating well after each addition.

Tint or color with liquid or paste food coloring if you wish. If the frosting is too soft, add a little more sugar and shortening and beat well.

CHAPTER 2

Seven Basic Layer Cakes and How to Decorate Them

YELLOW LAYER CAKE

BUTTER SPONGE LAYER CAKE

WHITE LAYER CAKE

SWEET CREAM LAYER CAKE AND SWEET CREAM MARBLE CAKE

CHOCOLATE LAYER CAKE

LEMON LAYER CAKE

BURNT SUGAR LAYER CAKE

The quintessential American cake is a layer cake, and a terrific layer cake with a great buttercream frosting is welcome anywhere, any time.

This chapter is devoted to basic layer cakes and what you can do with them: Following each recipe you'll find three sets of suggestions for fillings, frostings and simple no-piping decorations. If you are new to cake decorating, it's a good idea to read the general information on filling and frosting techniques in Chapter 1, pages 23–24. For more specific information about piping and other cake decorations, read the Decorating Primer on pages 25–30.

YELLOW LAYER CAKE

*MAKES TWO 8-INCH ROUND LAYERS OR ONE SMALL
SHEET CAKE PLUS ABOUT EIGHT MEDIUM CUPCAKES*

Every baker needs a basic yellow cake to rely on, and this is mine. It's quick and easy to prepare and makes the perfect foundation for almost any filling, frosting, fruit sauce or ice cream. This cake freezes well, too.

*BAKING PAN: TWO 8-INCH ROUND CAKE PANS OR ONE 11 × 7 × 1½-INCH
SHEET CAKE PAN PLUS ONE MEDIUM MUFFIN PAN*

*PAN PREPARATION: GREASE AND FLOUR CAKE PANS; LINE MUFFIN PANS
WITH PAPER BAKING CUPS*

PREHEAT OVEN TO 375°

*BAKING TIME: 20–25 MINUTES FOR 8-INCH LAYERS; 25 MINUTES FOR
SHEET CAKE; 20 MINUTES FOR CUPCAKES*

2½ cups cake flour	1½ cups sugar
3 teaspoons baking powder	2 eggs, beaten
1 teaspoon salt	2 teaspoons vanilla extract
½ cup (1 stick) butter, softened	1 cup milk

1. Stir or whisk together the flour, baking powder and salt; set aside.

2. In a large bowl, cream the butter until it is light. Add the sugar gradually, beating well after each addition.

3. Pour in the beaten eggs a little at a time, beating well after each addition. Add the vanilla and blend thoroughly.

4. Add the dry ingredients and the milk alternately, in three parts each, blending well after each addition.

5. If you are making round layers, pour equal amounts of batter into the two prepared pans. Bake for 20–25 minutes or until a cake tester inserted in the center of the cake comes out clean.

If you are making the small sheet cake and cupcakes, measure four scant cups of batter into the sheet cake pan and a scant ¼ cup of batter into each paper-lined muffin cup (about eight cupcakes). Bake both pans at the same time on the center rack of the oven, removing the cupcakes after 20 minutes and the sheet cake after 25 minutes or when a cake tester comes out clean.

Let round layers or cupcakes cool in the pans on wire racks for ten minutes; turn out and let them finish cooling right side up on the racks. Sheet cake may be cooled in the pan on a wire rack for ten minutes and then carefully turned out *or* it may be left in the pan to cool completely (and then frosted and served right from the pan).

6. When the layers (or sheet cake and cupcakes) are completely cool, fill and/or frost with your choice of filling and frosting or follow one of the suggestions given here. You'll also find some simple decorating ideas in the list opposite. For more decorating inspiration, see pages 25–29 in Chapter 1.

SUGGESTIONS FOR FILLING, FROSTING AND DECORATION

Filling and frosting: Spread layers with seedless raspberry jam and then with Mocha Buttercream Frosting (pages 163–164).

Decoration: Fresh raspberries *or* frozen raspberries, defrosted and drained

Filling and frosting: Orange Buttercream Frosting (page 164)

Decoration: Drizzle the top of the cake with a lattice of Brandy Glaze (page 173) and sprinkle with slivers of orange peel (how-to, page 25).

Easter Cake

Filling and frosting: Snowdrift Frosting (page 166), tinted pale yellow or pink

Decoration: Green coconut "grass"; candy eggs; jelly beans

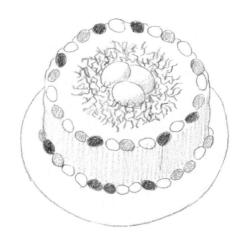

BUTTER SPONGE LAYER CAKE

MAKES THREE 8-INCH ROUND LAYERS
OR TWO 9-INCH ROUND LAYERS

Butter Sponge Layer Cake, also called *genoise*, is one of the most versatile, elegant layer cakes you can bake. Its fine texture and rich taste make it ideal for combining with fresh fruit, buttercream frosting, pastry cream, jams and preserves, marzipan, nuts or liqueur. In fact, butter sponge is often used as a base on which to build simple or complicated desserts; you will find it used here in Raspberries-and-Cream Cake (page 88) and Miniature Iced Cakes (page 134).

TIP: It is extremely important to let the eggs come to room temperature before using them in the recipe.

BAKING PAN: THREE 8-INCH ROUND CAKE PANS
OR TWO 9-INCH ROUND CAKE PANS

PAN PREPARATION: GREASE; LINE EACH PAN WITH A WAXED PAPER CIRCLE;
GREASE THE WAXED PAPER CIRCLES; DUST THE PANS WITH FLOUR

PREHEAT OVEN TO 350°

BAKING TIME: 25–30 MINUTES

1 cup flour	1 cup superfine sugar
¼ teaspoon salt	½ cup (1 stick) butter, clarified and
6 eggs, *room temperature*	cooled (see note before step 1)
1 teaspoon vanilla extract	

NOTE: To clarify butter, first melt the butter in a small saucepan over very low heat. Turn off the heat, pour the melted butter into a measuring cup or small pitcher and let the white milk solids settle for half an hour. Most of the solids will drift down to the bottom of the cup, but some may float. Use a little spoon to skim off the floating bits, then pour the clear, golden butter into a bowl and discard the solids left on the bottom of the cup.

1. Stir or whisk together the flour and salt; set aside.

2. In a large bowl, with an electric mixer, beat the eggs and vanilla until light and thick and quadrupled in volume.

Add the sugar one tablespoon at a time, beating continuously. Keep beating until the mixture is thick and airy, like soft whipped cream; when you lift the beaters, a thick rope of batter will fall and sit on top of the mixture for a few seconds before leveling out. Be sure to get the beaters way down into the bowl so all the batter is beaten equally.

NOTE: The amount of time it takes to beat the eggs and sugar to the proper consistency varies according to the power of your mixer; it may take from five to 20 minutes.

3. Use a fine strainer to sift about a quarter of the flour over the egg mixture. Fold in the flour very gently. Repeat until all the flour is incorporated.

4. Put the clarified butter and one cup of the batter into a separate bowl and whisk them together until well blended. Return this mixture to the main bowl of batter ¼ cup at a time, folding it in gently but thoroughly. Pour equal amounts of batter into the prepared pans.

5. Bake for 25–30 minutes, checking after 25 minutes. When the cake is done the top will be golden and will spring back when pressed lightly in the center; the cake will be pulling away from the sides of the pan.

Let the layers cool in the pans on wire racks for ten minutes. Run a knife around each layer. Turn out onto wire racks, peel off the waxed paper and turn the layers right side up on the racks to finish cooling.

6. When the layers are completely cool, fill and frost with your favorite flavor of buttercream frosting, pastry cream, sweetened whipped cream or pastry cream lightened with whipped cream. (Before frosting the layers, you may brush them with rum, sherry or liqueur and/or spread them with warmed strained jam or preserves.) Here are some specific filling and frosting suggestions.

SUGGESTIONS FOR FILLING, FROSTING AND DECORATION

Filling: Almond Pastry Cream (page 171)

Frosting: Almond Pastry Cream lightened with whipped cream

Decoration: Chocolate-dipped almonds

Filling and frosting: Spread layers with strained apricot jam and then with Basic Vanilla Buttercream Frosting (page 162).

Decoration: Drizzle the top of the cake with Mocha Glaze (page 173) or another favorite glaze.

Filling: Lemon Pastry Cream (page 171)

Frosting: Lemon Pastry Cream lightened with whipped cream *or* Lemon Buttercream Frosting (page 164)

Decoration: Thin slices of lemon and orange

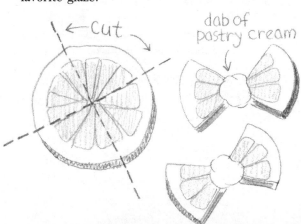

WHITE LAYER CAKE

*MAKES THREE 8-INCH ROUND LAYERS OR TWO 9-INCH
ROUND LAYERS OR ABOUT 28 MEDIUM CUPCAKES*

The taste and texture will remind you of angel food cake, but this white cake is richer and easier to make. The layers freeze well.

TIP: If you're feeling whimsical, tint the batter with a little food coloring—pink for a romantic occasion, pale green for St. Patrick's Day and so on.

*BAKING PAN: THREE 8-INCH ROUND CAKE PANS OR TWO 9-INCH ROUND
CAKE PANS OR ONE OR TWO MEDIUM MUFFIN PANS*

*PAN PREPARATION: GREASE AND FLOUR CAKE PANS;
LINE MUFFIN PANS WITH PAPER BAKING CUPS*

PREHEAT OVEN TO 350°

*BAKING TIME: 30 MINUTES FOR 8-INCH LAYERS; 35 MINUTES FOR
9-INCH LAYERS; 20 MINUTES FOR CUPCAKES*

2¾ cups cake flour
3 teaspoons baking powder
½ teaspoon salt
1 teaspoon vanilla extract

1 cup milk
10 tablespoons butter, softened
1¾ cups sugar
5 egg whites

1. Stir or whisk together the cake flour, baking powder and salt; set aside. In a measuring cup, stir the vanilla into the milk; set aside.

2. In a large bowl, cream the butter until light. Gradually add 1¼ cups of the sugar, beating well after each addition.

3. Add the milk and the dry ingredients alternately, in three parts each, blending well after each addition.

4. In a separate bowl, with clean, dry beaters, beat the egg whites until foamy. Add the remaining ½ cup of sugar one tablespoon at a time, beating constantly, until the egg whites stand in firm, glossy, moist peaks. Fold a third of the egg whites into the batter to lighten it; fold the remaining egg whites into the lightened batter.

Divide the batter equally between the prepared cake pans and spread it evenly in each pan; fill each paper baking cup with ¼ cup of batter.

5. Bake 8-inch layers for 30 minutes, 9-inch layers for 35 minutes and cupcakes for 20 minutes or until a cake tester inserted in the center of the cake comes out clean. The cake will be light brown on top and pulling away from the sides of the pan.

Let the cake cool in the pans on wire racks for ten minutes. Turn the layers or cupcakes out to finish cooling right side up on the racks.

For the cupcakes: If you have a second muffin pan prepared and filled with batter, put it in the oven as soon as you take out the first pan. If you are working with just one muffin pan, prepare and fill it again as soon as the first batch of cupcakes has been turned out. Bake and cool the second batch as described above.

6. When the layers or cupcakes are completely cool, fill and/or frost with your favorite filling and frosting or follow one of the suggestions given below. If you need decorating inspiration and instruction, see pages 25–29 in Chapter 1.

SUGGESTIONS FOR FILLING, FROSTING AND DECORATION

Filling and frosting: Snowdrift Frosting (page 166), tinted pink
Decoration: Red glacé cherries

Thanksgiving Cake
Filling and frosting: Spread layers with warmed orange marmalade or apricot jam and then with Lemon Buttercream Frosting (page 164).
Decoration: Press chopped nuts around the sides; place a few fresh chrysanthemums and leaves in the center.

Filling and frosting: Pineapple-Coconut Chunky Buttercream Frosting (page 163)
Decoration: Pineapple butterflies, made with well-drained canned pineapple slices and walnut halves, as shown

SWEET CREAM LAYER CAKE
AND SWEET CREAM MARBLE CAKE

*MAKES TWO 9-INCH ROUND LAYERS
OR ONE LARGE SHEET CAKE*

Heavy cream is used in this cake instead of butter, to make tender layers with a delicate flavor. The recipe converts easily from white cake to marble cake—see step 4.

The layers freeze well.

*BAKING PAN: TWO 9-INCH ROUND CAKE PANS
OR ONE 9 × 13 × 2-INCH SHEET CAKE PAN*

PAN PREPARATION: GREASE AND FLOUR

PREHEAT OVEN TO 350°

*BAKING TIME: 30 MINUTES FOR 9-INCH LAYERS;
35 MINUTES FOR SHEET CAKE*

2½ cups flour
2 teaspoons baking powder
½ teaspoon salt
3 eggs
2 teaspoons vanilla extract
1½ cups sugar
1½ cups heavy cream

For marble cake:
1 ounce (1 square) unsweetened chocolate, melted and cooled
1 tablespoon unsweetened cocoa powder

1. Stir or whisk together the flour, baking powder and salt; set aside.

2. In a large bowl, beat the eggs for several minutes, until they are light, thick and pale. Add the vanilla and beat again.

3. Add the sugar one tablespoon at a time, beating well after each addition.

4. Add the dry ingredients and the cream alternately, in three parts each. After each addition, beat just until blended.

For plain sweet cream layers: Divide the batter equally between the two prepared pans or spread all the batter in the prepared sheet cake pan.

For marble sweet cream layers: Put half the batter in a separate bowl. To one bowl of batter add the melted chocolate and the cocoa powder and blend well. Drop alternating spoonfuls of dark and light batter into each prepared pan, ending up with equal amounts of batter in each pan. To make the marbled effect, draw a knife back and forth through the dark and light batter several times; do not overdo the marbling or you will get a muddy-looking cake.

5. Bake 9-inch layers for 30 minutes and sheet cake for 35 minutes or until a cake tester inserted in the center of the cake comes out clean.

Let the layers cool in the pans on wire racks for ten minutes; turn them out to finish cooling right side up on the racks. Let the sheet cake cool completely in the pan on a wire rack (and then frost and serve it right from the pan) *or* let it cool in the pan on a wire rack for ten minutes and then carefully turn it out to finish cooling on the rack.

6. When the layers or sheet cake are completely cool, fill and/or frost with your choice of filling and frosting or follow one of the suggestions given here. You will also find some simple decorating ideas in the list below. For decorating inspiration, see pages 25–29 in Chapter 1.

SUGGESTIONS FOR FILLING, FROSTING AND DECORATION

Filling and frosting: Lemon Buttercream Frosting (page 164)

Decoration: Strawberry halves; banana slices; mandarin orange slices, drained and dried

Filling: Mocha Buttercream Frosting (page 163), mixed with chopped glacé chestnuts

Frosting: Mocha Buttercream Frosting

Decoration: Glacé chestnuts

Mother's Day Cake

Filling: Almond Pastry Cream (page 171)

Frosting: Basic Vanilla Buttercream Frosting (page 162), tinted peach-color

Decoration: Small nosegay of spring flowers tied with satin ribbon, placed off-center on top of cake

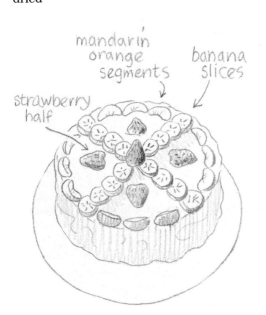

mandarin orange segments

banana slices

strawberry half

CHOCOLATE LAYER CAKE

MAKES THREE 8-INCH ROUND LAYERS OR TWO
9-INCH ROUND LAYERS OR ABOUT 36 MEDIUM
CUPCAKES OR ONE LARGE SHEET CAKE

A good basic chocolate cake is almost as versatile as a basic yellow cake. The ingredients for these chocolate layers are a little different from what you might expect in a basic cake, but I've stretched the point because this one is so delicious.

TIP: Consider making just two 8-inch layers for a dessert cake plus a dozen or so cupcakes to wrap individually and store in the freezer for brown bag lunches.

BAKING PAN: THREE 8-INCH ROUND CAKE PANS OR
TWO 9-INCH ROUND CAKE PANS OR ONE OR TWO MEDIUM MUFFIN PANS
OR ONE 9 × 13 × 2-INCH SHEET CAKE PAN

PAN PREPARATION: GREASE AND FLOUR ROUND CAKE PANS
OR SHEET CAKE PAN; LINE MUFFIN PANS WITH PAPER BAKING CUPS

PREHEAT OVEN TO 350°

BAKING TIME: 35 MINUTES FOR 8-INCH LAYERS; 40 MINUTES FOR 9-INCH
LAYERS; 25 MINUTES FOR CUPCAKES; 50 MINUTES FOR SHEET CAKE

1½ cups flour
1½ cups cake flour
6 tablespoons unsweetened cocoa
    powder
1½ teaspoons baking soda
1½ teaspoons salt

¾ cup (1½ sticks) butter, softened
2 cups sugar
3 eggs, beaten
¼ cup coffee
1½ cups sour cream

1. Stir or whisk together the flour, cake flour, cocoa powder, baking soda and salt; set aside.

2. In a large bowl, cream the butter until light. Gradually add the sugar, beating well after each addition.

3. Pour in the beaten eggs a little at a time, beating well after each addition. When all the eggs are incorporated, beat for two more minutes at medium speed.

4. Add the coffee and blend well.

5. Add the dry ingredients and the sour cream alternately, in three parts each, blending well after each addition. Divide the batter equally between the prepared round cake pans *or* put a scant ¼ cup of batter in each paper-lined muffin cup *or* spread all the batter in the sheet cake pan.

6. Bake 8-inch layers for 35 minutes, 9-inch layers for 40 minutes, cupcakes for 25 minutes and sheet cake for 50 minutes or until a cake tester inserted in the center of the cake comes out clean.

Let the cake cool in the pans or wire racks for ten minutes. Turn the layers or cupcakes out and let them finish cooling right side up on the racks. Sheet cake may either be cooled completely in the pan on a wire rack (and frosted and served directly from the pan) *or* carefully turned out to finish cooling right side up on the rack.

For the cupcakes: If you have a second muffin pan prepared and filled with batter, put it in the oven as soon as you take out the first pan. If you are working with just one muffin pan, prepare and fill it again as soon as the first batch of cupcakes has been turned out. Bake and cool the second batch as described above.

7. When the layers, cupcakes or sheet cake are completely cool, fill and/or frost with your favorite filling and frosting or follow one of the suggestions given below. If you need decorating inspiration and instruction, see pages 25–29 in Chapter 1.

SUGGESTIONS FOR FILLING, FROSTING AND DECORATION

Father's Day Cake
   Filling and frosting: Cream Cheese Frosting (page 169)
   Decoration: Spell out DAD with chocolate chips in the center of a ring of really good filled chocolates.

   Filling: Coffee Pastry Cream (page 171)
   Frosting: Easy Chocolate Buttercream Frosting (page 163)
   Decoration: Press chocolate sprinkles into the sides of the cake; top the frosted cake with dollops of Coffee Pastry Cream and more chocolate sprinkles.

   Filling and frosting: Chocolate-Nut Chunky Buttercream Frosting (page 163), made with white chocolate and chopped almonds
   Decoration: Chocolate-dipped almonds

LEMON LAYER CAKE

MAKES TWO 8-INCH ROUND LAYERS
OR ONE LARGE SHEET CAKE

For the lemon mavens—a delicate cake that gets its real lemon flavor from fresh lemon juice and freshly grated lemon rind.

TIP: Don't fudge on the ingredients; bottled lemon juice and dried lemon peel are not acceptable substitutes.

BAKING PAN: TWO 8-INCH ROUND CAKE PANS
OR ONE 9 × 13 × 2-INCH SHEET CAKE PAN

PAN PREPARATION: GREASE AND FLOUR

PREHEAT OVEN TO 375°

BAKING TIME: 25 MINUTES FOR LAYERS OR SHEET CAKE

2 cups cake flour
1½ teaspoons baking powder
1 teaspoon baking soda
¼ teaspoon salt
½ cup milk

3 tablespoons fresh lemon juice
1 tablespoon grated lemon rind
½ cup (1 stick) butter, softened
1 cup sugar
3 eggs, beaten

1. Stir or whisk together the cake flour, baking powder, baking soda and salt; set aside. In a measuring cup, stir together the milk, lemon juice and grated lemon rind (the mixture will curdle); set aside.

2. In a large bowl, cream the butter until light. Add the sugar gradually, beating well after each addition.

3. Pour in the beaten eggs a little at a time, beating well after each addition.

4. Add the dry ingredients and the milk mixture alternately, in three parts each, blending well after each addition. Pour equal amounts of batter into the two prepared round pans or pour all the batter into the prepared sheet cake pan.

5. Bake the layers or the sheet cake for 25 minutes or until a cake tester inserted in the center of the cake comes out clean.

Let the layers cool in the pans on wire racks for ten minutes and then turn them out to finish cooling right side up on the racks. Let the sheet cake cool completely in the pan on a wire rack (and frost and serve straight from the pan) *or* let it cool for ten minutes in the pan on a wire rack and then carefully turn it out to finish cooling right side up on the rack.

6. When the layers or sheet cake are completely cool, fill and/or frost with your favorite filling and frosting or follow one of the suggestions listed opposite. For decorating instructions and ideas, turn to pages 25–29 in Chapter 1.

SUGGESTIONS FOR FILLING, FROSTING AND DECORATION

Filling and frosting: Orange Buttercream Frosting (page 164), tinted pale yellow or peach-color

Decoration: Seedless grapes (red and/or green)

Filling and frosting: Creamy Chocolate Frosting (page 167)

Decoration: Dollops or piped rosettes of sweetened whipped cream, topped with whole hazelnuts or almonds

Filling and frosting: Sour Cream Frosting (page 169)

Decoration: Slivers of lemon peel (how-to, page 25)

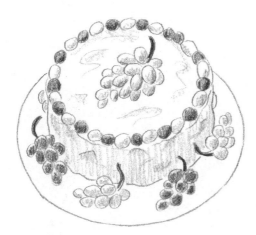

BURNT SUGAR LAYER CAKE

*MAKES TWO 8-INCH ROUND LAYERS OR ONE SMALL
SHEET CAKE AND FIVE OR SIX MEDIUM CUPCAKES*

This old-fashioned cake is made with a burnt sugar syrup that gives it a beautiful amber color and a warm, light caramel flavor. The cake freezes well.

*BAKING PAN: TWO 8-INCH ROUND CAKE PANS OR ONE 11 × 7 × 1½-INCH
SHEET CAKE PAN PLUS ONE MEDIUM MUFFIN PAN*

*PAN PREPARATION: GREASE AND FLOUR CAKE PANS;
LINE MUFFIN PAN WITH PAPER BAKING CUPS*

PREHEAT OVEN TO 375°

*BAKING TIME: 25–30 MINUTES FOR 8-INCH LAYERS; 35 MINUTES FOR
SHEET CAKE; 20–25 MINUTES FOR CUPCAKES*

For the caramel syrup:
½ cup sugar
½ cup boiling water

For the batter:
2 cups flour
2½ teaspoons baking powder
½ teaspoon baking soda
½ teaspoon salt
½ cup sugar
½ cup light brown sugar
½ cup (1 stick) butter, softened
1 teaspoon vanilla extract
2 eggs, beaten
¾ cup milk

1. Make the caramel syrup: Put the ½ cup of sugar in an 8-inch skillet over medium heat. Cook, stirring, until the sugar melts and turns first golden and then a darker amber. This will happen just as the sugar begins to boil. Remove the skillet from the heat.

Very carefully, add the boiling water, *one tablespoonful at a time,* stirring constantly with a long-handled spoon; the hot syrup will bubble up, so stand back from the pan. Return the skillet to low heat and cook the syrup for a few minutes, stirring constantly, until all the lumps and stickiness have dissolved.

Pour the syrup into a measuring cup and set aside to cool; you should have ½–⅔ cup of syrup.

2. Stir or whisk together the flour, baking powder, baking soda and salt; set aside. In another bowl, stir the white and brown sugars together; set aside.

3. In a large bowl, cream the butter until light. Add the combined sugars gradually, beating well after each addition.

4. Stir the vanilla into the beaten eggs. Pour the eggs into the creamed mixture a little at a time, beating well after each addition. After the eggs have been incorporated, beat for another three minutes at medium speed. By the time you finish, the mixture should be quite light and most of the sugar dissolved.

5. Add the caramel syrup a little at a time, beating continuously.

6. Add the dry ingredients and the milk alternately, in three parts each, blending well after each addition.

7. If you are making round layers, pour equal amounts of batter into the two prepared pans. Bake for 25–30 minutes or until a cake tester inserted in the center of the cake comes out clean.

If you are making the small sheet cake plus cupcakes, pour four cups of batter into the sheet cake pan (filling it about halfway) and a scant ¼ cup of batter into each paper-lined muffin cup (about five cupcakes). Bake both pans on the center rack of the oven at the same time, removing the cupcakes after 20–25 minutes and the sheet cake after 35 minutes or when a cake tester inserted in the center comes out clean.

Let round layers or cupcakes cool in the pans for ten minutes on wire racks; turn out and let them finish cooling right side up on the wire racks. Sheet cake may be cooled in the pan on a wire rack for ten minutes and then carefully turned out to finish cooling *or* it may be left in the pan on the wire rack to cool completely (and then frosted and served right from the pan).

8. When the layers or sheet cake and cupcakes are completely cool, fill and/or frost with your favorite filling and frosting or follow one of the suggestions below. If you need some help with decorating ideas and instructions, turn to pages 25–29 in Chapter 1.

SUGGESTIONS FOR FILLING, FROSTING AND DECORATION

Filling and frosting: Coconut Pecan Caramel Frosting (page 165)
Decoration: Whole pecans and chocolate chips

Filling: Coffee Pastry Cream (page 171)
Frosting: Coffee Pastry Cream lightened with whipped cream
Decoration: Dollops or piped rosettes of whipped cream

Halloween Cake
Filling and frosting: Basic Vanilla Buttercream Frosting (page 162), tinted orange
Decoration: Candy corn; licorice strings; raisins; chocolate sprinkles

candy corn

licorice strings & chocolate sprinkles

raisins

OTHER LAYER CAKES TO MAKE:

Light Chocolate Cake with Creamy Chocolate Frosting and Crisp Almond
  Macaroons, page 50
Banana Layer Cake, page 99
Fresh Coconut Layer Cake, page 108
Holiday Jam Cake with Sugarplums, page 144
Gingerbread Cottage, page 155

CHAPTER 3

Fabulous Chocolate Cakes

CHOCOLATE BROWNIE CAKE WITH
DOUBLE CHOCOLATE FROSTING

CHOCOLATE POUND CAKE

LIGHT CHOCOLATE CAKE WITH CREAMY CHOCOLATE
FROSTING AND CRISP ALMOND MACAROONS

CHOCOLATE ALMOND SAND CAKE

SOUTH AMERICAN CHOCOLATE CAKE

STRAWBERRY-CROWNED DEVIL'S FOOD CAKE
WITH SOUR CREAM FROSTING

CHOCOLATE CHEESECAKE WITH
CHERRY TOPPING

MOCHA SPONGE ROLL WITH CHESTNUT FILLING
AND CHOCOLATE GLAZE

These chocolate cakes, like chocolate bars, run the gamut of flavors from dark to milk chocolate and range in style from simple to elaborate. There is something here for every chocolate-lover.

It may surprise and delight you to learn that for baking these chocolate cakes, our own standard American brands of baking chocolate are the equals of the expensive imported brands. Therefore, when recipes call for squares of baking chocolate, unsweetened cocoa powder and chocolate chips, buy the high-quality, brand name products available in the supermarket—the same ones that you and your mother and grandmother have always used.

CHOCOLATE BROWNIE CAKE
WITH DOUBLE CHOCOLATE FROSTING

MAKES ONE SMALL SHEET CAKE

A tender, brownie-like cake studded with lots of chopped pecans and generously spread with fudgy chocolate frosting. Perfect for afternoon snacks, school birthday parties and Sunday suppers.

TIP: This cake is rather fragile, so handle it carefully when transferring it from wire rack to serving platter.

BAKING PAN: ONE 11 × 7 × 1½-INCH SHEET CAKE PAN

PAN PREPARATION: GREASE AND FLOUR

PREHEAT OVEN TO 350°

BAKING TIME: 35–40 MINUTES

1 cup flour
2 teaspoons baking powder
3 tablespoons unsweetened cocoa powder
¼ teaspoon salt
6 tablespoons butter, softened
1¼ cups sugar
3 eggs, separated
1½ teaspoons vanilla extract

3 ounces (3 squares) unsweetened chocolate, melted and cooled
6 tablespoons milk
1 cup chopped pecans

For the frosting and decoration:
½ recipe Double Chocolate Frosting (page 167)
Chopped pecans

1. Stir or whisk together the flour, baking powder, cocoa powder and salt; set aside.

2. In a large bowl, cream the butter until light. Gradually add one cup of the sugar, beating well after each addition.

3. Add the egg yolks one at a time, beating well after each addition. Add the vanilla and blend well.

4. Add the melted chocolate and blend well.

5. Add the dry ingredients and milk alternately, in three parts each, beating well after each addition. Stir the chopped nuts into the batter.

6. In another large bowl, with clean, dry beaters, beat the egg whites until foamy. Add the remaining ¼ cup of sugar and beat until the egg whites stand in firm, glossy, moist peaks. Fold half of the egg whites into the batter to lighten it; fold the rest of the egg whites into the lightened batter.

Pour the batter into the prepared pan and spread it evenly.

7. Bake for 35–40 minutes or until a cake tester inserted in the center of the cake comes out clean. Let the cake cool completely in the pan on a wire rack.

8. Run a sharp knife around the sides of the cake and invert it onto another wire rack. Remove the pan, cover the cake with an inverted serving platter and flip the rack, cake and platter so that the cake is right side up on the platter. Do this carefully because the cake is fragile.

Frost with Double Chocolate Frosting and immediately sprinkle chopped pecans on the frosting.

CHOCOLATE POUND CAKE

MAKES ONE 9-INCH RING

A firm, moist, dark chocolate cake. If you like your chocolate straight, just eat this cake as it is; I like it best with a little Vanilla Glaze (page 172) drizzled on while the cake is still warm.

BAKING PAN: ONE 9-INCH FLUTED TUBE PAN, 3¾ INCHES DEEP
PAN PREPARATION: GREASE AND FLOUR
PREHEAT OVEN TO 325°
BAKING TIME: 80–90 MINUTES

5 ounces (5 squares) unsweetened
   chocolate
1¼ cups milk
2 cups flour
2 teaspoons baking powder
1 teaspoon salt

3 eggs
1½ teaspoons vanilla extract
9 tablespoons butter, softened
2 cups sugar

Vanilla Glaze (page 172; optional)

1. Put the chocolate and the milk in a small saucepan and stir constantly over low heat until the chocolate melts and blends with the milk. Set aside to cool to lukewarm.

Stir or whisk together the flour, baking powder and salt; set aside. In another bowl, beat the eggs with the vanilla; set aside.

2. In a large bowl, beat together the butter and sugar until well blended; the mixture will be grainy. Add the lukewarm chocolate mixture and beat until smooth and glossy.

3. Add the egg mixture and beat again. Gradually add the dry ingredients, beating well after each addition. Pour the batter into the prepared pan.

4. Bake for 80–90 minutes or until a cake tester inserted in the cake comes out clean. Let the cake cool in the pan on a wire rack for ten minutes and then turn the cake out to finish cooling rounded side up on the rack.

If desired, drizzle Vanilla Glaze over the warm cake.

LIGHT CHOCOLATE CAKE WITH CREAMY CHOCOLATE FROSTING AND CRISP ALMOND MACAROONS

MAKES A TWO-LAYER ROUND CAKE

Light Chocolate Cake belongs at the milk chocolate end of the chocolate spectrum—light and mellow in both texture and flavor. It's a cake that still tastes delicious several days after baking, when the macaroons are soft and the frosting has moistened the cake.

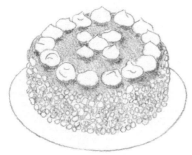

BAKING PAN: TWO 9-INCH ROUND CAKE PANS
PAN PREPARATION: GREASE AND FLOUR
PREHEAT OVEN TO 350°
BAKING TIME: 30 MINUTES

1¾ cups cake flour
2 teaspoons baking powder
¼ teaspoon baking soda
1 teaspoon salt
1½ cups sugar
½ cup (1 stick) butter, melted and
  cooled

1¼ cups evaporated milk
1 teaspoon vanilla extract
2 eggs
2 ounces (2 squares) unsweetened
  chocolate, melted and cooled

Crisp Almond Macaroons (recipe
  follows on page 51; see step 1)
Creamy Chocolate Frosting (page
  167; see step 5)

1. Make the Crisp Almond Macaroons according to the recipe on page 51 and set them aside.

2. In a large bowl, stir or whisk together the cake flour, baking powder, baking soda, salt and sugar. Add the melted butter and one cup of the evaporated milk and beat just until all the dry ingredients are moistened.

3. Add the remaining ¼ cup of evaporated milk, the vanilla, eggs and melted chocolate and blend well. Divide the batter equally between the two prepared pans.

4. Bake for 30 minutes or until a cake tester inserted in the center of the cake comes out clean. Let the layers cool in the pans on wire racks for ten minutes and then turn them out to finish cooling right side up on the racks.

While the cake cools, make the Creamy Chocolate Frosting.

5. Assemble the finished cake as follows: Set aside 20 of the prettiest macaroons for decorating the top of the cake. Put the remaining macaroons in a plastic bag and use a rolling pin to crush them into small pieces (not crumbs).

Put one layer of the cake on a serving platter and tuck strips of waxed paper under the cake to protect the platter (how-to, page 24).

Stir together one heaping cup of Creamy Chocolate Frosting and ¾ cup of macaroon pieces. Spread this on the first layer.

Cover with the second layer and spread all the remaining frosting on the top and sides of the cake. Decorate the top of the cake with the reserved whole macaroons, as shown in the drawing at the beginning of the recipe, and pat macaroon pieces onto the sides of the cake. Refrigerate the cake for one hour and then remove the waxed paper strips.

Refrigerate until serving time.

CRISP ALMOND MACAROONS

MAKES ABOUT 60 SMALL COOKIES

BAKING PAN: TWO COOKIE SHEETS
PAN PREPARATION: GREASE AND FLOUR
PREHEAT OVEN TO 275°
BAKING TIME: 30 MINUTES

2 egg whites
¼ teaspoon vanilla extract
¼ teaspoon almond extract
Pinch of cream of tartar

Pinch of salt
½ cup sugar
¾ cup ground toasted almonds,
blanched or unblanched

1. Put the egg whites, vanilla, almond extract, cream of tartar and salt in a large bowl and beat until the egg whites hold soft peaks.

Add the sugar, one tablespoon at a time, beating until the egg whites hold firm, glossy, moist peaks and all the sugar is dissolved.

2. Fold in the ground almonds.

3. Spoon the batter into a sturdy plastic bag and push it down to one corner of the bag. Twist the bag closed just above the batter. Snip off a small piece of the corner to make a hole ½–¾-inch in diameter.

Pipe the batter through the hole onto one cookie sheet, making approximately 30 small mounds of about one heaping teaspoonful each. Leave an inch between mounds. When one cookie sheet is full, pipe 30 mounds onto the second sheet.

4. Bake one sheet at a time, for 30 minutes per sheet. Let the macaroons cool completely on the cookie sheet on a wire rack; they will become crisp as they cool. Remove the cooled macaroons one at a time by twisting each one off the cookie sheet; do *not* use a spatula.

CHOCOLATE ALMOND SAND CAKE

MAKES ONE 8-INCH SQUARE CAKE

A "sandy" cake has a delicate, slightly crumbly texture made by using ground nuts and cornstarch in the batter. This small cake has a light chocolate-and-almond flavor enhanced by Mocha Buttercream Frosting. Decorate the top with whole or slivered toasted almonds.

BAKING PAN: ONE 8-INCH SQUARE CAKE PAN (BROWNIE PAN)
PAN PREPARATION: GREASE AND FLOUR
PREHEAT OVEN TO 325°
BAKING TIME: 35–40 MINUTES

4 ounces (4 squares) semisweet chocolate
3 tablespoons milk or cream
⅓ cup flour
¾ cup sifted cornstarch
Pinch of salt
3 eggs, separated
1 whole egg
10 tablespoons sugar

½ cup ground almonds
6 tablespoons butter, melted and cooled

For the frosting and decoration:
1⅓ cups Mocha Buttercream Frosting (page 163)
Whole or slivered toasted almonds

1. Put the chocolate and the milk or cream in a small saucepan over low heat, stirring until melted and smooth; set aside to cool.

Stir or whisk together the flour, cornstarch and salt; set aside.

2. In a large bowl, beat together the three egg yolks and the whole egg until thickened and pale. Add nine tablespoons of the sugar, one tablespoon at a time, beating continuously until the mixture is even thicker and paler.

3. Stir in the ground almonds and the chocolate mixture and blend well.

4. Fold in the dry ingredients a little at a time.

5. In another large bowl, with clean, dry beaters, beat the three egg whites until foamy. Add the remaining tablespoon of sugar and beat until the whites stand in firm, glossy, moist peaks. Fold the egg whites into the chocolate batter.

6. Fold the melted butter into the batter. Pour the batter into the prepared pan.

7. Bake for 35–40 minutes or until a cake tester inserted in the center of the cake comes out clean. Let the cake cool in the pan on a wire rack for ten minutes and then turn the cake out to finish cooling right side up on the rack.

8. Transfer the cake to a serving platter and tuck strips of waxed paper under it (how-to, page 24). Frost the top and sides with Mocha Buttercream Frosting. Decorate the top with whole or slivered almonds.

SOUTH AMERICAN CHOCOLATE CAKE

MAKES ONE 9-INCH RING

My grandmother, Blanche Small, loves coffee. Perhaps that's why she has been making this rich coffee-laced cake for so many years. It has a wonderfully moist texture, created by adding a surprising ingredient— old-fashioned oats.

BAKING PAN: ONE 9-INCH FLUTED TUBE PAN, 3¾ INCHES DEEP

PAN PREPARATION: GREASE AND FLOUR

PREHEAT OVEN TO 350°

BAKING TIME: 55–60 MINUTES

1¼ cups hot black coffee
1 cup uncooked old-fashioned (not instant) oats
1½ cups flour
1 teaspoon baking soda
½ teaspoon salt
½ cup (1 stick) butter, softened
1½ cups sugar
1 teaspoon vanilla extract

2 eggs, beaten
2 ounces (2 squares) unsweetened chocolate, melted and cooled
1 cup semisweet chocolate chips

Vanilla Glaze (optional; page 172)
or Mocha Glaze (optional; page 173)

1. Pour the hot coffee over the oats in a small saucepan. Stir to mix, cover the pan and set aside for 20 minutes.

Stir or whisk together the flour, baking soda and salt; set aside.

2. In a large bowl, cream the butter until light. Gradually add the sugar, beating well after each addition.

3. Stir the vanilla into the beaten eggs and pour the eggs into the creamed mixture a little at a time, beating well after each addition.

4. Add the melted chocolate and blend well. Add the oats mixture and blend again. The batter will have a rather odd, gluey texture at this point, but don't be concerned about it.

5. Gradually stir the dry ingredients into the batter, blending well. Add the chocolate chips and stir again. Pour the batter into the prepared pan.

6. Bake for 55–60 minutes or until a cake tester inserted in the cake comes out free of batter. (The cake tester may pierce a melted chocolate chip and come out coated with chocolate, so test in several spots to confirm that the cake is done.)

Let the cake cool in the pan on a wire rack for ten minutes and then turn the cake out to finish cooling rounded side up on the rack.

Drizzle with Vanilla or Mocha Glaze if desired.

STRAWBERRY-CROWNED DEVIL'S FOOD CAKE WITH SOUR CREAM FROSTING

MAKES A THREE-LAYER SQUARE CAKE

A typically American combination of flavors—the cake is all-American devil's food, the filling is a blend of cut-up strawberries and Sour Cream Frosting and the topping is Sour Cream Frosting with beautiful chocolate-dipped strawberries for decoration.

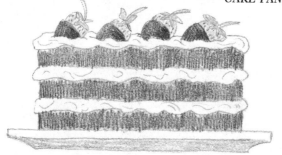

BAKING PAN: TWO OR THREE 8-INCH SQUARE CAKE PANS (BROWNIE PANS); SEE STEP 5

PAN PREPARATION: GREASE

PREHEAT OVEN TO 325°

BAKING TIME: 25 MINUTES

For the decoration:
32 strawberries
3 ounces (3 squares) semisweet
   chocolate
1 teaspoon vegetable oil

For the batter:
4 ounces (4 squares) unsweetened
   chocolate
¼ cup (½ stick) butter
½ cup milk

1½ tablespoons white or cider
   vinegar
1½ teaspoons baking soda
2 cups flour
1 teaspoon salt
2 cups sugar
2 eggs
2 teaspoons vanilla extract
1 cup boiling water

Sour Cream Frosting (page 169)

1. Prepare the chocolate-dipped strawberries for decorating the top of the cake: Rinse all the berries, pat them as dry as possible on paper towels and then let them air-dry *completely*.

In a small saucepan over low heat, melt the semisweet chocolate with the oil, stirring until smooth. Pick out 16 perfect

berries and dip each berry about halfway into the melted chocolate, holding it by the stem or leaves. Set the chocolate-dipped berries on waxed paper; it will take about two hours for the chocolate to harden. Discard the leftover melted chocolate.

Hull the remaining berries and cut them into quarters for the filling; set aside.

2. Melt the unsweetened chocolate and the butter in a small saucepan over low heat. Stir well and transfer to a large bowl; set aside to cool.

In a small bowl, stir together the milk, vinegar and baking soda and set aside for five minutes; the mixture will foam up quickly. In another bowl, stir or whisk together the flour and salt; set aside.

3. Beat the milk mixture into the cooled chocolate mixture. Add the sugar and beat at high speed for one minute.

4. Add the eggs and vanilla and beat at high speed for another minute.

5. Add the dry ingredients and the boiling water alternately, in three parts each, beating well at high speed after each addition.

Measure the batter. If you have three prepared pans, pour equal amounts of batter into each of them. If you have only two pans to work with, pour one third of the batter into each pan and reserve the remaining batter to bake when the first two pans come out of the oven (see step 6).

6. Bake for 25 minutes or until a cake tester inserted in the center of the cake comes out clean. Let the layers cool in the pans on wire racks for ten minutes. Turn them out to finish cooling right side up on the racks.

NOTE: If you can't fit all three pans on the center rack of the oven, bake two layers and then—when they are done— bake the third layer. If you are working with only two pans, you must wait to bake the third layer until the first two layers are baked, cooled and turned out of the pans. Then wash one pan, grease it, fill it with the remaining batter and bake as described above.

7. While the cake is baking and cooling, make the Sour Cream Frosting, if you haven't done so already. Put two cups of frosting in a bowl, add the cut-up strawberries and stir to make the filling. Set aside the remaining cup of frosting for the top of the cake.

8. Assemble the cake: First, if any layer is not fairly flat, level the top with a sharp knife.

Put one layer on a serving platter and spread half of the filling on it. Cover with a second cake layer and spread the remaining filling on that layer. Add the third layer and press gently to make a firm stack.

Spread the reserved cup of Sour Cream Frosting on the top layer. Carefully lift each chocolate-dipped strawberry from the waxed paper and press in place on the frosting, as shown in the drawing. Serve immediately or refrigerate until half an hour before serving.

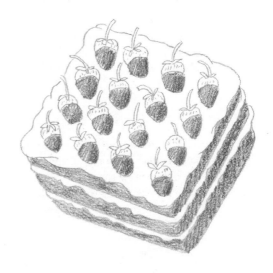

CHOCOLATE CHEESECAKE WITH CHERRY TOPPING

MAKES ONE 9-INCH CAKE

I find that this cake yields twelve to sixteen servings because it is so rich and satisfying that only a few hardy souls can eat more than a thin wedge.

BAKING PAN: ONE 9-INCH SPRINGFORM PAN

PAN PREPARATION: GREASE

PREHEAT OVEN TO 450°

BAKING TIME: 45 MINUTES OF BAKING; TOTAL OF TWO HOURS AND 45 MINUTES IN THE OVEN

For the crust:
1½ cups chocolate wafer crumbs (about 26 chocolate wafer cookies)
¾ cup ground pecans
½ cup (1 stick) butter, melted and cooled

For the filling:
2 tablespoons unsweetened cocoa powder
1 tablespoon flour
½ teaspoon salt
½ cup sugar

½ cup light brown sugar
1½ pounds (three 8-ounce packages) cream cheese, softened
5 eggs
2 teaspoons vanilla extract
1 cup sour cream
8 ounces (8 squares) semisweet chocolate, melted and cooled

For the topping:
Three 8¾-ounce cans of dark, sweet, pitted cherries
2 tablespoons vodka or kirsch
1 teaspoon cornstarch

1. Make the crust: Stir together the cookie crumbs, ground pecans and melted butter. Put the mixture in the prepared springform pan and pat it out to cover the bottom of the pan evenly; set the pan aside.

2. Stir or whisk together the cocoa powder, flour, salt and sugars; set aside.

3. In a large bowl, beat the softened cream cheese until it is very smooth. Add the cocoa mixture and beat again until smooth.

4. Add the eggs one at a time, beating well after each addition. Stir in the vanilla and sour cream and then the melted chocolate. Be sure the mixture is thoroughly blended.

Pour and spoon the filling onto the crust in the springform pan.

5. Bake for 15 minutes at 450°. Reduce the oven temperature to 300° and continue baking for 30 minutes more.

Turn off the heat but *leave the cheese-cake in the oven* to continue baking in the residual heat for one more hour. At the end of the hour, *do not remove the cheesecake from the oven:* Prop open the oven door just a little, using the handle of a wooden spoon, and leave the cheesecake in the slowly cooling oven for another hour.

Now remove the cheesecake from the oven; it has been in the oven for a total of two hours and 45 minutes. If it is not completely cool, let it finish cooling in the pan on a wire rack.

NOTE: By this time, your cheesecake may have developed some major or minor cracks on top. Don't worry about them because the cherry topping will conceal them very effectively.

Carefully run a knife around the cake to loosen it and then release and remove the sides of the springform pan. Leave the cheesecake on the bottom of the pan and refrigerate it while you make the topping.

6. Drain the cherries over a small saucepan. Set the cherries aside for now. There should be about one cup of liquid in the saucepan.

Add the vodka or kirsch to the cherry liquid and stir. Put one tablespoon of the mixture in a small bowl with the cornstarch and blend well; set aside for now. Cook the cherry liquid over low heat until it is reduced to about ¾ cup. Add the cornstarch mixture and continue cooking, stirring constantly, until thick. Add the reserved cherries and stir well. Turn off the heat and let the cherry topping cool.

When the topping is cool, arrange the cherries neatly on top of the cheesecake. If there is any syrup left in the saucepan, drizzle it over the cherries.

Return the cheesecake to the refrigerator to chill. Half an hour before serving, take the cake out of the refrigerator. Run a long metal spatula under the crust to loosen the cake from the bottom of the pan and carefully slide the cheesecake onto a flat platter.

Serve at room temperature.

MOCHA SPONGE ROLL WITH CHESTNUT FILLING AND CHOCOLATE GLAZE

MAKES ONE ROLL ABOUT TEN INCHES LONG

There are three parts to this cake—the delicate sponge roll, the rich filling and the smooth glaze. None is difficult to make, but they do take some time, so I would call this a special-occasion cake.

Don't shy away from making this just because you've had no success with rolled cakes before. Follow the instructions carefully and you'll have no trouble.

BAKING PAN: ONE 10½ × 15½ × 1-INCH JELLY ROLL PAN

PAN PREPARATION: GREASE; LINE COMPLETELY (BOTTOM AND SIDES) WITH WAXED PAPER; GREASE THE WAXED PAPER

PREHEAT OVEN TO 350°

BAKING TIME: 12–14 MINUTES

½ cup sifted cake flour
3 tablespoons unsweetened cocoa powder
¼ teaspoon salt
2 tablespoons hot coffee
1 tablespoon instant coffee granules
1 teaspoon vanilla extract
5 eggs, separated
½ cup sugar
Confectioners' sugar

Chestnut Filling (recipe follows on page 60)

For the topping:
½ recipe Semisweet Chocolate Glaze (page 172)
Chopped walnuts or chopped pistachios

1. Stir or whisk together the flour, cocoa and salt; set aside. In another bowl, stir together the hot coffee, instant coffee granules and vanilla; set aside.

2. In a large bowl, beat the egg yolks until they are thickened and pale. Add the sugar one tablespoon at a time, beating well after each addition. When all the sugar is incorporated, continue beating at high speed for two more minutes, until the mixture is very thick.

3. Add the coffee mixture and stir it in gently. Add the dry ingredients in four approximately equal parts, blending just until thoroughly moistened.

4. In a separate bowl, with clean, dry beaters, beat the egg whites until they stand in firm, glossy, moist peaks. Fold a third of the whites into the batter to lighten it; fold the remaining egg whites into the lightened batter.

Working quickly, spread the batter evenly in the prepared pan, especially into the corners. Put it in the oven without delay so the egg whites don't lose volume.

5. Bake for 12–14 minutes or until a cake tester inserted in the center of the cake comes out clean. Do not overbake.

While the cake is baking, get out a clean linen or other lint-free dish towel and a wire rack or cookie sheet larger than the jelly roll pan.

When the cake is done, take the pan out of the oven. Working quickly, cover the pan first with the dish towel and then with the inverted rack or cookie sheet. Flip the pan, towel and rack or cookie sheet to turn out the cake. Remove the pan and then slowly and carefully peel off the waxed paper.

Slide the towel and cake onto the table or counter; the cake is wrong side up. Cut off any crisp edges and sift a little confectioners' sugar over the cake. Fold one end of the towel over the short end of the cake and roll the cake up in the towel.

Place the rolled cake seam side down on the wire rack to cool.

6. When the cake is cool, unroll it and spread Chestnut Filling evenly over the entire cake.

Roll up the cake again, this time without the towel (but using the towel to help roll), and place it seam side down on a serving platter. Refrigerate the filled roll for 30 minutes to firm the filling before you trim the ends and add the glaze.

7. Take the filled roll out of the refrigerator and trim a thin slice from each end. Tuck strips of waxed paper under the roll (how-to, page 24) and drizzle generously with Semisweet Chocolate Glaze. Before the glaze sets, sprinkle the chopped nuts on the top and pat chopped nuts on the sides of the roll. Let the glaze set and then remove the waxed paper strips.

Refrigerate until half an hour before serving.

CHESTNUT FILLING

MAKES ABOUT TWO CUPS

One 8-ounce jar of whole chestnuts
¼ **cup cognac or brandy**
¼ **cup (½ stick) butter, softened**

One 3-ounce package cream cheese,
   softened
¾ **cup confectioners' sugar**

1. Drain the chestnuts and put them in the bowl of a food processor fitted with the steel chopping blade. Add the cognac or brandy and process until the mixture is smooth and paste-like.

2. Add the remaining ingredients and process until smooth, scraping down the bowl several times. Transfer the filling to a small bowl.

The filling should be a perfect spreading consistency, but if it is too thick, add another tablespoon of cognac or brandy and blend well.

OTHER CHOCOLATE CAKES TO MAKE:

Chocolate Layer Cake, page 40
Mississippi Mud Cake, page 98

Chocolate Grand Marnier Torte, page 140
Yule Log, page 158

CHAPTER 4

Pound Cakes, Tea Loaves and Snack Cakes

PERFECT POUND CAKE AND VARIATIONS

BUTTERMILK LEMON POUND CAKE

ALMOND TEA CAKES

APRICOT-ORANGE OR CURRANT-ORANGE TEA LOAVES

DARK SWEET DATE-NUT LOAF

PECAN SPICE LOAVES

BEST CARROT CAKE SQUARES

These are homey, friendly cakes, easy to make and quick to disappear. They are generally prepared with simple, readily available ingredients and baked in just one pan. Very little frosting or decorating is required—the cake itself is the important thing.

Turn to this chapter when you want to whip up a tasty afternoon snack or a simple dessert. Individual servings of these cakes can be wrapped in plastic and tucked into brown bag lunches.

PERFECT POUND CAKE AND VARIATIONS

MAKES ONE LOAF OR ONE TUBE CAKE

Perfect pound cake should be in every baker's basic repertoire. Delicious by itself, it can also be sliced and dressed up to make any number of special desserts: Add fresh fruit and whipped cream; crown with a scoop of ice cream and a sprinkling of nuts; brush with liqueur and top with a spoonful of pastry cream. In addition, the variations given here will change a basic pound cake into Almond, Marble or Rum Raisin Pound Cake.

BAKING PAN: ONE 9½ × 5½ × 2¾-INCH LOAF PAN OR ONE 10½-INCH TUBE PAN, THREE INCHES DEEP

PAN PREPARATION: GREASE AND FLOUR

PREHEAT OVEN TO 325°

BAKING TIME: 70–80 MINUTES FOR THE LOAF; 50–60 MINUTES FOR THE TUBE CAKE

2 cups flour
½ teaspoon baking powder
¼ teaspoon salt
¼ teaspoon nutmeg
5 eggs
½ teaspoon vanilla extract
1 cup (2 sticks) butter, softened
1½ cups sugar

For Rum Raisin Pound Cake:
¾ cup dark raisins soaked in
    ⅓ cup rum for 1½ hours

For Marble Pound Cake:
omit nutmeg
3 tablespoons unsweetened cocoa
    powder

For Almond Pound Cake:
omit vanilla extract
½ teaspoon almond extract
¾ cup finely chopped toasted
    almonds

1. Stir or whisk together the flour, baking powder, salt and nutmeg (omit nutmeg if you are making Marble Pound Cake); set aside. In another bowl, beat the eggs with the vanilla (or with the almond extract if you are making Almond Pound Cake); set aside.

2. In a large bowl, cream the butter until light. Add the sugar one tablespoon at a time, beating well after each addition.

When all the sugar is incorporated, beat for another two minutes at medium speed.

3. Add the egg mixture a little at a time, beating well at medium speed after each addition. (The mixture will stiffen and then, as you beat in more eggs, will become thinner.) By the time you finish, the mixture will be pale and light and all the sugar will have dissolved. Beat at high speed for one more minute.

4. Add the dry ingredients ⅓ cup at a time, sprinkling them over the batter and folding them in. Be sure all the dry ingredients are incorporated after each addition.

If you are making Perfect Pound Cake, *proceed to step 5*. If you are making one of the variations, follow the instructions below.

For Rum Raisin Pound Cake: Drain the raisins well. Stir them gently into the batter. *Proceed to step 5*.

For Marble Pound Cake: Transfer one-fourth of the batter to a small bowl. Add the cocoa powder, sifting it through a fine strainer, and stir well to make chocolate batter. Fill the prepared pan with the batters, alternating large spoonfuls of light batter with small spoonfuls of chocolate batter. Draw a knife through the filled pan three or four times to create the marbling. *Proceed to step 6*.

For Almond Pound Cake: Gently stir the chopped almonds into the batter. *Proceed to step 5*.

5. Pour or spoon the batter into the prepared pan. If you are making a loaf cake, push the batter well into the corners and slightly higher on the sides than in the center; this helps prevent uneven baking and a mountainous rise in the center of the cake.

6. Bake the loaf cake for 70–80 minutes and the tube cake for 50–60 minutes or until a cake tester inserted in the cake comes out clean.

NOTE: The Rum Raisin Pound Cake may take a little longer to bake.

Let the cake cool in the pan on a wire rack for ten minutes and then turn out to finish cooling right side up on the rack.

BUTTERMILK LEMON POUND CAKE

MAKES ONE 10½-INCH TUBE CAKE

One of the best pound cakes you'll ever taste—a sensational combination of rich, lemony cake and tart-sweet lemon syrup. This recipe makes a large cake so it's great for a crowd.

BAKING PAN: ONE 10½-INCH TUBE PAN, THREE INCHES DEEP
(DO NOT USE A SMALLER PAN)

PAN PREPARATION: GREASE AND FLOUR

PREHEAT OVEN TO 325°

BAKING TIME: 65–75 MINUTES

For the lemon syrup:
¾ cup water
¾ cup sugar
3 tablespoons fresh lemon juice

For the batter:
3 cups flour
½ teaspoon baking soda

¼ teaspoon salt
1 cup (2 sticks) butter, softened
2¼ cups sugar
5 eggs
1 teaspoon vanilla extract
1 tablespoon fresh lemon juice
2 teaspoons grated lemon rind
1 cup buttermilk

1. Make the lemon syrup: Put the water, sugar and lemon juice in a small, heavy saucepan. Bring to a boil and stir to dissolve the sugar. Lower the heat and simmer until the mixture is reduced to ¾ cup. Set aside.

2. Stir or whisk together the flour, baking soda and salt; set aside.

3. In a large bowl, cream the butter and sugar. Add the eggs one at a time, beating well after each addition.

4. Add the vanilla, lemon juice and grated lemon rind and blend well.

5. Add the dry ingredients and the buttermilk alternately, in three parts each, blending well after each addition. Pour or spoon the batter into the prepared pan and spread it evenly.

6. Bake for 65–75 minutes or until a cake tester inserted in the cake comes out clean. (The cake will rise impressively during baking but will not overflow the sides of the pan.) Let the cake cool in the pan on a wire rack for ten minutes and then turn it out to finish cooling rounded side up on the rack.

7. While the cake is still very warm, brush lemon syrup all over it. Repeat several times, waiting a few minutes between coats, until all the syrup is used up. When all the syrup is absorbed and the outside of the cake is just slightly sticky, carefully transfer the cake to a serving platter.

ALMOND TEA CAKES

MAKES 18 SMALL CAKES

Made with cornstarch as well as flour and ground almonds, these firm little cupcakes have a sandy, melt-in-your-mouth texture and a delicate taste.

TIP: Best when eaten completely cooled and spread with butter, on the same day they are baked; freeze any leftovers, but expect the defrosted cakes to be just a bit dry.

BAKING PAN: ONE OR TWO MEDIUM MUFFIN PANS

PAN PREPARATION: GREASE AND FLOUR OR LINE WITH PAPER BAKING CUPS

PREHEAT OVEN TO 350°

BAKING TIME: 15–20 MINUTES

1 cup flour
½ cup cornstarch
½ cup ground almonds
   NOTE: Grind the almonds to a crumb-like consistency; do not grind to a powder.
¼ teaspoon salt

¾ cup (1½ sticks) butter, softened
¾ cup sugar
3 eggs
½ teaspoon vanilla extract
½ teaspoon almond extract
2 tablespoons cream
Chopped or slivered almonds

1. Stir or whisk together the flour, cornstarch, ground almonds and salt; set aside.

2. In a large bowl, cream the butter and sugar until light.

3. Add the eggs one at a time, beating well after each addition. Add the vanilla, almond extract and cream and beat well.

4. Add the dry ingredients: Sprinkle a spoonful of the flour mixture evenly over the egg mixture and fold it in gently with a spatula. Repeat until all the flour mixture is incorporated.

Fill each cup of the prepared muffin pan half-full of batter and top each filled cup with a few chopped or slivered almonds.

NOTE: If you have a second muffin tin, fill those cups now, too. Set aside until the first pan is finished baking, unless your oven is large enough to accommodate both pans side by side on the center rack.

5. Bake for 15–20 minutes, checking after 15 minutes; the cakes are done if they are firm when pressed in the center. Let the cakes cool in the pan on a wire rack for ten minutes, then remove and let them finish cooling on the rack.

If you do not have a second muffin pan ready to go, wash, dry and prepare the first pan and repeat the filling and baking process to make the rest of the tea cakes.

Serve with butter when the cakes are completely cool.

APRICOT-ORANGE OR CURRANT-ORANGE TEA LOAVES

*MAKES THREE MINIATURE LOAVES OR ONE
MINIATURE LOAF PLUS ONE REGULAR LOAF*

Make these tea loaves with dried apricots for a slightly tangy cake or with dried currants for a sweeter, mellower taste. In either case, the cake has a distinct orange flavor, a buttery richness and a lovely crumb. The miniature loaves make excellent gifts.

*BAKING PAN: THREE 6 × 3 × 2-INCH MINIATURE LOAF PANS OR ONE
MINIATURE LOAF PAN PLUS ONE 9½ × 5½ × 2¾-INCH LOAF PAN*

PAN PREPARATION: GREASE AND FLOUR

PREHEAT OVEN TO 425°

BAKING TIME: 25–30 MINUTES

¾ cup chopped dried apricots *or*
¾ cup dried currants (see note
before step 1)
Flour for coating the fruit
(see step 1)
2 cups flour
2 teaspoons baking powder
½ teaspoon salt

½ cup (1 stick) butter
¾ cup sugar
3 eggs
½ cup milk
1 scant tablespoon grated orange
rind
½ cup orange juice

NOTE: Use good-quality, firm-textured apricots. If they are hard, soak in very hot water just long enough to soften them; remove them from the water before they get mushy. Drain and dry on paper towels. Do *not* soak the currants.

1. Spread the chopped apricots or the currants in one layer on a piece of waxed paper. Sprinkle with a little flour and toss with your fingers to coat them lightly. Be sure all the bits are separated so there are no clumps.

Stir together the two cups of flour, the baking powder and salt. Add the apricots or currants and stir again; set aside.

2. In a large bowl, cream the butter and sugar. Add the eggs one at a time, beating well after each addition.

3. Add the flour mixture and the milk alternately, in three parts each, blending well after each addition.

4. Add the grated orange rind and the orange juice to the batter, blending well. Pour the batter into the prepared pans, filling each one just a bit more than half full.

5. Put the pans on the center rack of the oven and bake for 25–30 minutes or until a cake tester inserted in the center of each loaf comes out clean.

Let the loaves cool in the pans on wire racks for ten minutes. Run a knife around each loaf and then turn them all out to finish cooling right side up on the racks.

DARK SWEET DATE-NUT LOAF

MAKES ONE LOAF

This recipe comes to me from Ruth Abrams and I am grateful for it. Mrs. Abrams's family won't eat any other date-nut bread—try it yourself and you'll understand why they feel so strongly.

BAKING PAN: ONE 9½ × 5½ × 2¾-INCH LOAF PAN
PAN PREPARATION: GREASE AND FLOUR
PREHEAT OVEN TO 350°
BAKING TIME: 55–60 MINUTES

1 cup pitted, sliced dates (see note before step 1)
¾ cup coarsely chopped walnuts
1½ teaspoons baking soda
½ teaspoon salt
¾ cup boiling water

3 tablespoons solid white vegetable shortening
2 eggs
1 teaspoon vanilla extract
1 cup sugar
1½ cups flour

NOTE: Slice each date in four pieces. This is easy to do if the dates are cold and the knife is rinsed in hot water.

1. Put the sliced dates and chopped nuts in a large bowl. Sprinkle the baking soda and the salt over them and mix well with your fingers, breaking up any clumps of dates. Add the boiling water and the shortening and stir until the shortening is completely melted. Set the mixture aside for 20 minutes.

2. Beat together the eggs and vanilla. In another bowl, stir the sugar and flour together.

3. Add the beaten eggs to the cooled date mixture and stir well. Add the dry ingredients and stir just until blended. Pour and spoon the batter into the prepared pan.

4. Bake for 55–60 minutes or until a cake tester inserted in the center of the loaf comes out free of batter (although it may have some sticky date clinging to it).

Let the loaf cool in the pan on a wire rack for ten minutes and then turn it out to finish cooling right side up on the rack.

Serve warm or cool, with butter or cream cheese.

PECAN SPICE LOAVES

MAKES TWO LOAVES

You'll get rave reviews from the spice cake lovers for this moist, tender, nut-filled loaf. It is not overly sweet, but "sweet" spices like cinnamon increase the perception of sweetness without added sugar.

TIP: The nuts are important in this cake so be sure to use really fresh pecans with no trace of staleness.

BAKING PAN: TWO 8½ × 4½ × 2½-INCH LOAF PANS

PAN PREPARATION: GREASE AND FLOUR

PREHEAT OVEN TO 350°

BAKING TIME: 45 MINUTES

2 cups flour	½ cup (1 stick) butter,
1 teaspoon baking soda	softened
¼ teaspoon salt	1 cup sugar
2 teaspoons cinnamon	½ cup light brown sugar
½ teaspoon nutmeg	3 eggs, separated
½ teaspoon allspice	1 cup sour cream
¼ teaspoon ground cloves	1½ cups chopped pecans

1. Stir or whisk together the flour, baking soda, salt and spices; set aside.

2. In a large bowl, cream the butter and white sugar until light. Gradually add the brown sugar, beating well after each addition.

3. Add the egg yolks and beat thoroughly.

4. Add the dry ingredients and the sour cream alternately, in three parts each, blending well after each addition.

5. Stir in the chopped pecans.

6. In another large bowl, with clean, dry beaters, beat the egg whites until they hold firm, glossy, moist peaks. Gently fold one-fourth of the egg whites into the batter to lighten it; fold the rest of the egg whites into the lightened batter.

Pour equal amounts of batter into the prepared pans.

7. Bake for 45 minutes or until a cake tester inserted in the center of each loaf comes out clean. Let the loaves cool in the pans on wire racks for five minutes, then turn the loaves out to finish cooling on the racks.

BEST CARROT CAKE SQUARES

MAKES ABOUT 24 SQUARES

Chopped pecans and golden raisins (substituted for the usual walnuts and dark raisins) make all the difference to this superior carrot cake. Frost lavishly with traditional Cream Cheese Frosting and serve right from the pan. Because it's large, this cake is good for a crowd.

BAKING PAN: ONE 9 × 13 × 2-INCH SHEET CAKE PAN

PAN PREPARATION: GREASE AND FLOUR

PREHEAT OVEN TO 350°

BAKING TIME: 55–60 MINUTES

2 cups flour
2 teaspoons baking powder
1 teaspoon baking soda
½ teaspoon salt
1½ teaspoons cinnamon
1 cup chopped pecans
1 cup golden raisins
1 cup (2 sticks) margarine, softened

1 cup sugar
1 cup light brown sugar
1 teaspoon vanilla extract
4 eggs, beaten
3 cups grated raw carrots (about
   one pound, peeled)

Cream Cheese Frosting (page 169)

1. Stir or whisk together the flour, the baking powder, baking soda, salt and cinnamon. Add the chopped pecans and stir; set aside.

Spread the raisins on a piece of waxed paper and sprinkle with a little additional flour. Toss with your fingers to coat the raisins lightly; set aside.

2. In a large bowl, cream the margarine and white sugar. Add the brown sugar gradually, beating until the mixture is light.

3. Stir the vanilla into the beaten eggs. Add the eggs to the creamed mixture a little at a time, beating well after each addition.

4. Gradually add the dry ingredients, blending thoroughly after each addition. Stir the raisins into the batter.

5. Stir the grated carrots into the batter a handful at a time, blending after each addition. Pour the batter into the prepared pan and spread it evenly.

6. Bake for 55–60 minutes or until a cake tester inserted in the center of the cake comes out clean. The cake will be quite brown on top.

Let the cake cool in the pan on a wire rack. When the cake is completely cool, frost it with Cream Cheese Frosting and serve it right from the pan.

OTHER POUND CAKES, TEA LOAVES AND SNACK CAKES TO MAKE:

Chocolate Pound Cake, page 49
Blueberry Buttermilk Spice Squares, page 89
Cranberry-Filled Lemon Loaf, page 90
Pineapple Upside-Down Cake, page 103

CHAPTER 5

Yeast Coffeecakes and Quick Coffeecakes

BASIC YEAST DOUGH FOR COFFEECAKES
AND SMALL PASTRIES

FILLED VIENNA BRAID AND FILLED RING

FOLDED POCKETS AND BEAR CLAWS

QUICK RICH LITTLE COFFEECAKES

RAISIN BRAN BATTER CAKE

HONEY PECAN PULL-APARTS

CINNAMON PRUNE YOGURT CAKE

PEACH AND BLUEBERRY KUCHEN

Yeast coffeecakes are made from sweet, yeast-leavened dough, with the addition of nuts, fruit fillings and glazes. The dough must be kneaded and allowed to rise, usually twice. Working with yeast dough is a delightful experience because the dough feels so lively and warm in your hands—and because it produces such professional-looking results.

Quick coffeecakes are made from sweet batter leavened with baking powder and/or baking soda, enhanced with fresh or dried fruit, spices and jam. Quick coffeecakes are easy to make because the batter is simply mixed and poured straight into the baking pans.

BASIC YEAST DOUGH FOR COFFEECAKES AND SMALL PASTRIES

*MAKES TWO COFFEECAKES OR ONE COFFEECAKE
PLUS 9–18 SMALL PASTRIES OR 18–36 SMALL PASTRIES*

This slightly sweet dough works perfectly with sweet fillings and glazes to make filled coffeecakes, and it also makes lovely plain braids for those who prefer simpler cakes. My favorite pairings of fillings and glazes are listed below; use any of these three combinations for any of the coffeecakes or small pastries described here.

1. Prune Filling, Tart Lemon Glaze
2. Almond Filling, Butterscotch Glaze
3. Apricot Filling, Cream Glaze

You'll find the filling and glaze recipes on pages 76–77, at the end of the yeast dough recipe.

TIP: The amounts of butter, sugar and egg in this dough make it a slow riser, but give it sufficient time and it will rise properly.

BAKING PAN: ONE OR TWO COOKIE SHEETS

PAN PREPARATION: GREASE

PREHEAT OVEN TO 350° AFTER DOUGH HAS RISEN TWICE

*BAKING TIME: 20 MINUTES FOR COFFEECAKES;
15 MINUTES FOR SMALL PASTRIES*

¼ cup warm water (see step 1)
1 package (¼ ounce; scant table-
    spoon) dry yeast
½ cup milk
¼ cup (½ stick) butter, softened
½ cup sugar
1 teaspoon salt

3–3½ cups flour
1 egg, beaten

For the egg wash:
1 egg
1 tablespoon sugar
1 tablespoon milk or cream

1. Prepare the yeast: You need warm water at the right temperature—105° to 115°—to activate the yeast properly, so first fill a measuring cup with warm water and test it with an instant-reading thermometer. Adjust the temperature by pouring off some water and then adding either hot or cold water until the thermometer reads between 105° and 115°. The water should feel definitely warm to the fingertips, not hot or cool. When you have the correct temperature, pour off all but ¼ cup of water and test again.

Sprinkle the yeast over the warm water and stir with a warmed spoon to dissolve the yeast; set aside.

2. Scald the milk. Turn off the heat, add the butter and stir to melt it. Pour the mixture into a large bowl. Add the sugar and salt and stir to dissolve the sugar. Allow the mixture to cool to a reading of 110° or less on the instant-reading thermometer; it should feel warm to the fingertips.

3. Add 1½ cups of flour and mix well to make a batter.

4. Stir the yeast mixture again to be sure the yeast is thoroughly dissolved. Add the yeast mixture and the beaten egg to the batter and blend well.

5. Blend in another 1½–2 cups of flour, half a cup at a time, to make a soft, somewhat shaggy ball of dough that is not too sticky. Turn the dough out onto a floured surface. Dust your hands with flour and knead the dough until it is smooth and elastic, about ten minutes. Dust the surface and your hands often with flour to keep the dough from sticking.

6. Grease a large bowl with butter or margarine and put the ball of kneaded dough in the bowl; turn the dough all around to coat it with a film of butter or margarine. Cover the bowl with a clean dish towel and place it in a draft-free spot (for example, the oven with no heat on) for the dough to rise until doubled in size, about 2½–3 hours.

This first rising takes quite some time, since the yeast needs time to work on the rich dough. Don't be concerned if the rising takes a little longer than three hours.

7. Turn the dough out onto a floured surface and punch it down. Let it rest for ten minutes and then divide it in half. Shape and fill each half to make the coffeecakes and/or small pastries you have chosen. The shaping instructions are on pages 74–76.

NOTE: If at any time during the shaping process the dough resists being rolled, let it rest for a few minutes and then continue.

Cover the unbaked coffeecakes and/or pastries with the dish towel and allow to rise again in a draft-free spot until puffy, about 1½–2 hours. The dough will not double in size but it will be noticeably larger.

8. Whisk together the ingredients for the egg wash. Brush the tops and sides of the unbaked coffeecakes and small pastries with egg wash.

Bake the small pastries for 15 minutes and the coffeecakes for 20 minutes; they should be golden brown on top.

NOTE: If you are using more than one cookie sheet, bake one at a time on the middle rack of the oven.

Let the coffeecakes and pastries cool on the cookie sheet on a wire rack for ten minutes. Run a long spatula under them to loosen them and then cool for ten more minutes on the cookie sheet. *Slide* the cakes and *lift* the pastries off the cookie sheet and transfer to the racks to finish cooling.

9. While the coffeecakes and pastries are still warm, drizzle or brush glaze on them. You may also pour a thick river of glaze down the center of any warm coffeecake. Remember that all the glazes given here will set and form a crust very quickly.

NOTE: Leftover glaze may be refrigerated and saved for later use. Bring it to room temperature before using it; if it has become very thick, thin it with a bit of the appropriate liquid.

These coffeecakes and pastries tend to get stale rather quickly, so be sure to freeze any that you are not planning to eat on baking day. To freeze, wrap individually in plastic; after defrosting, freshen them by warming gently in the oven.

FILLED VIENNA BRAID

From step 7, page 73:

On a floured surface roll out half of the dough to a 10 × 14-inch rectangle. Fold in thirds, as shown, and transfer to a prepared cookie sheet. Open the dough out again and reshape if necessary. Use a pastry wheel to cut the two outer sections into strips. Cut off a little bit of the last strip as shown.

Spread one cup of filling on the center section, not quite all the way to the ends of the dough. Fold the cut strips over the filling, alternating one strip from each side. The braid is most attractive if a little filling shows between the strips. Pinch each end together to enclose the filling.

Continue with step 7 (page 73) to complete the second rising, step 8 for baking and step 9 for glazing.

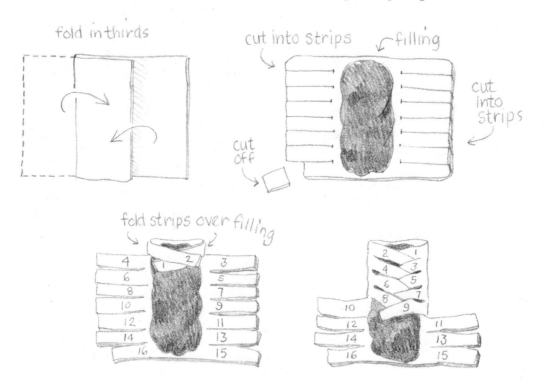

FILLED RING

From step 7, page 73:

On a floured surface roll out half of the dough to a 12 × 14-inch rectangle. Spread ¾ cup of filling over the rectangle, almost to the edges. Roll up from one long side, ending seam side down. Transfer the roll to a prepared cookie sheet and shape it into a ring, keeping the seam side down. Cut ½ inch off each end and join the cut ends by dampening them and pinching them together.

Use scissors to cut part way through the ring at one-inch intervals as shown.

Turn each section partly to the side to reveal the spiral of filling in each slice.

Continue with step 7 (page 73) to complete the second rising, step 8 for baking and step 9 for glazing.

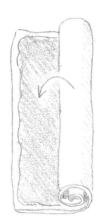

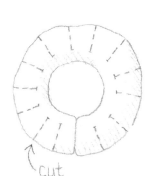

FOLDED POCKETS

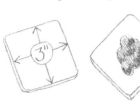

From step 7, page 73:

On a floured surface, roll out half the dough to a 9 × 18-inch rectangle. Use a pastry wheel to cut the rectangle into 3-inch squares. Put a heaping teaspoon of filling on each square, spread it slightly with the back of the spoon and fold two opposite corners over the filling as shown. Be sure the corners overlap about an inch or they may pop open during baking; the egg wash (step 8) will help secure them.

Transfer the pockets to a prepared cookie sheet, leaving about 1½ inches between them. Continue with step 7 (page 73) to complete the second rising, step 8 for baking and step 9 for glazing.

BEAR CLAWS

From step 7, page 73:

On a floured surface, roll out half the dough to a 12 × 18-inch rectangle. Spread ½ cup of filling evenly on the center section of the dough as shown below. Fold one side of the dough over the filling and spread ⅓ cup of filling on top of that. Fold the second side of the dough over the filling. Turn the flat roll over so that the seam side

is down. With a pastry wheel cut the roll in nine 2-inch pieces. Cut three slits in each piece as shown and transfer all the pieces to a prepared cookie sheet, leaving two inches between pieces. Fan out each piece to separate the "claws."

Continue with step 7 (page 73) to complete the second rising, step 8 for baking and step 9 for glazing.

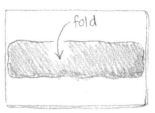

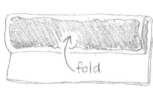

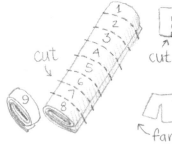

PRUNE FILLING

MAKES 1¼ CUPS

1 cup pitted prunes
2 tablespoons orange juice
1 teaspoon fresh lemon juice
1 tablespoon sugar
½ teaspoon almond extract

Put the prunes in a saucepan with water to cover and simmer until soft. Drain and let them cool slightly. While the prunes are still warm, purée them with the remaining ingredients in a food processor or blender until the mixture is smooth. Let the filling cool to room temperature before using.

TART LEMON GLAZE

MAKES ABOUT ½ CUP

2 tablespoons fresh lemon juice
1 teaspoon water
1 teaspoon grated lemon rind
1½ cups confectioners' sugar

Stir all the ingredients together and beat until smooth. If necessary, add a bit more water to thin the glaze or a bit more confectioners' sugar to thicken it.

ALMOND FILLING

MAKES ABOUT 1½ CUPS

1 cup blanched, toasted whole
    almonds (how-to, page 17)
1 cup confectioners' sugar
1 egg
3 tablespoons butter, softened

    Grind the toasted almonds in a food
processor or nut grater; do not let them
turn to paste. Stir the ground almonds and
sugar together. Add the egg and the butter
and blend well.

APRICOT FILLING

MAKES 1¼ CUPS

1 cup dried apricots
2 tablespoons fresh lemon juice
¼ cup sugar

    Put the apricots in a saucepan with
water to cover and simmer until soft. Drain
and let them cool slightly. While the apricots
are still warm, purée them with the other
ingredients in a food processor or blender
until the mixture is smooth. Let the filling
cool to room temperature before using.

BUTTERSCOTCH GLAZE

MAKES ABOUT ⅔ CUP

2 tablespoons butter
¼ cup light brown sugar
pinch of salt
3 tablespoons heavy cream
1 cup sifted confectioners' sugar

    Combine all the ingredients except
the confectioners' sugar in a heavy saucepan
and cook, stirring, over low heat until the
butter and brown sugar are completely
melted. Remove the pan from the heat and
let the mixture cool until it is just warm.
Add the confectioners' sugar and beat until
smooth.

CREAM GLAZE

MAKES ABOUT ONE CUP

2 cups confectioners' sugar, sifted
¼ cup heavy cream
2 teaspoons vanilla extract

    Heat the cream (do not boil) and beat
with the other ingredients until smooth and
well blended. If necessary, add a bit more
cream to thin the glaze.

QUICK RICH LITTLE COFFEECAKES

MAKES ABOUT 14 SMALL CAKES

This is my grandmother's recipe, the one that really sold me on baking when I was still a small child. The recipe hasn't lost one bit of its charm in the years since I first made it all by myself.

TIP: The cakes freeze well but should be warmed up to freshen them after defrosting.

BAKING PAN: COOKIE SHEET
PAN PREPARATION: GREASE
PREHEAT OVEN TO 375°
BAKING TIME: 25 MINUTES

2 cups flour
3 teaspoons baking powder
2 tablespoons sugar
½ teaspoon salt
½ cup (1 stick) cold butter, cut in pats
1 egg, beaten
⅔ cup milk

For the filling:
2 tablespoons very soft butter
½ cup apricot jam, warmed
1 cup chopped walnuts, pecans or a combination of both
1 cup dark raisins
¼ cup sugar mixed with a teaspoon of cinnamon

1. In a large bowl, stir or whisk together the flour, baking powder, the two tablespoons of sugar and the salt.

2. Add the pats of cold butter and cut them into the flour mixture until the mixture looks like fine crumbs.

NOTE: The easiest way to accomplish this is in a food processor fitted with the steel chopping blade, but you can do it very well by hand with a pastry blender.

3. Stir together the beaten egg and milk and add them to the flour mixture. Blend just until all the dry ingredients are moistened. Turn the dough out onto a floured surface and knead 30 strokes.

4. Dust the surface with flour again and roll out the dough to a 12 × 21-inch rectangle. Cover the dough with the filling ingredients as follows: First, use a blunt knife to spread the soft butter evenly over the dough. Next, with a pastry brush, spread a thin layer of warm apricot jam over the butter. Now sprinkle the dough evenly with the chopped nuts, then with the raisins and finally with the cinnamon-sugar mixture.

5. Carefully roll up the dough from the long side, ending with the seam side down. Mark the roll in 1½-inch sections and use a sharp knife to slice through the roll at the marks; this should make about 14 small cakes. Between cuts, wipe the knife and transfer each slice to the prepared cookie sheet, placing the slices upright as shown in the drawing above. Leave an inch between slices on the cookie sheet.

6. Bake for 25 minutes. The cakes will be golden brown on top and the filling may be oozing out a bit. Using a spatula, immediately transfer the cakes to a wire rack. Let them cool slightly and serve warm.

RAISIN BRAN BATTER CAKE

MAKES ONE 9-INCH RING

Warm or cool, this snack cake made with raisin bran cereal has a "golden brown" flavor—toasty, mellow and mildly sweet. Try it with butter, honey, peanut butter or all three.

TIP: The sweetness of this cake depends in part on the brand of cereal you choose. The "health food" brands are usually made with less sugar than the major brands and yield a slightly less sweet cake.

BAKING PAN: ONE 9-INCH FLUTED TUBE PAN, 3¾ INCHES DEEP

PAN PREPARATION: GREASE

PREHEAT OVEN TO 350°

BAKING TIME: 55–60 MINUTES

1½ cups raisin bran cereal
2 eggs
1½ cups milk
½ teaspoon almond extract
3 cups flour
½ cup sugar
½ cup dark brown sugar

3 teaspoons baking powder
¼ teaspoon baking soda
½ teaspoon salt
¾ cup raisins (golden, dark or a combination of both)
6 tablespoons butter, melted

1. Put the cereal in a plastic bag and use your hand to crush the flakes to small pieces; do not crush to powder. Set aside.

Beat together the eggs, milk and almond extract; set aside.

2. In a large bowl, stir together the crushed cereal, flour, both sugars, baking powder, baking soda, salt and the ¾ cup of raisins. Add the egg mixture and stir just until the dry ingredients are moistened.

3. Slowly pour in the melted butter while mixing just enough to blend. Pour the batter into the prepared pan.

4. Bake for 55–60 minutes or until a cake tester inserted in the cake comes out clean. The cake will be golden brown on top and pulling away from the sides slightly.

Let the cake cool in the pan on a wire rack for ten minutes, then turn it out to finish cooling right side up on the rack.

HONEY PECAN PULL-APARTS

MAKES 11 BUNS

You may know this yeast coffeecake recipe better as sticky buns, pecan rolls or even schnecken—honey-and-pecan-filled spirals that are baked as one round cake, then inverted and pulled apart into delectable individual servings.

BAKING PAN: ONE 9-INCH ROUND CAKE PAN

PAN PREPARATION: GREASE

PREHEAT OVEN TO 350° AFTER THE DOUGH HAS RISEN TWICE

BAKING TIME: ONE HOUR

For the filling:
¾ cup honey
½ cup dark corn syrup
1½–2 cups chopped pecans
¼ cup (½ stick) butter, softened

For the dough:
¼ cup warm water (see step 2)
1 package (¼ ounce; scant table-
    spoon) dry yeast
5 tablespoons milk
¼ cup (½ stick) butter, melted and
    kept warm
½ cup sugar
1 teaspoon salt
2 eggs, beaten
3–3¼ cups flour

1. Prepare the filling: Stir together the honey, corn syrup and chopped pecans until completely blended. Set aside this mixture and the softened butter.

2. Prepare the yeast: To activate the yeast, you must dissolve it in water with a temperature between 105° and 115°. First fill a measuring cup with warm water and test with an instant-reading thermometer. Adjust the temperature by pouring off some water and then adding either hot or cold water until the thermometer reads between 105° and 115°. The water should feel definitely warm on your fingertips, not hot or cool. When you have the correct temperature, pour off all but ¼ cup of water and test again.

Sprinkle the yeast over the warm water and stir with a warmed spoon to dissolve the yeast. Set aside for five minutes.

3. Scald the milk in a small saucepan and pour it into a large bowl. Add the warm melted butter and the sugar and stir until most of the sugar is dissolved. Add the salt and beaten eggs and blend well.

Add the dissolved yeast and blend again.

4. Add three cups of the flour, one cup at a time, mixing well after each addition. Add as many as four more tablespoons of flour, if needed, to make a soft but not sticky dough.

Turn the dough out onto a floured surface and knead for five minutes, until the dough is smooth and elastic. Dust the surface and your hands often with flour, to keep the dough from sticking.

Grease a medium-size bowl with butter and put the ball of dough in it, turning the dough to coat it with a film of butter. Cover the bowl with a clean dish towel and put it in a draft-free place (like the oven with the heat off) to rise for 2–2½ hours or until nearly doubled in size.

5. Turn the dough out onto a floured surface and punch it down. Let it rest for five minutes. While the dough is resting, spread half of the honey mixture in the bottom of the prepared pan.

Dust the dough with flour and roll it out to a 12 × 18-inch rectangle. Spread the softened butter on the dough almost to the edges. Spread the remaining honey mixture over the butter.

NOTE: The honey mixture is thick and rather difficult to spread, so drop it by spoonfuls on the buttered dough and then gently work it around with a knife to make an even layer.

Roll up the dough from the long side, ending with the seam side down. Use a serrated knife to mark the roll in 11 approximately equal pieces and slice through the roll at the marks, wiping the knife between cuts. Place the slices flat in the prepared pan as shown in the drawing.

For the second rising, turn on the oven for about ten seconds, just to warm it up a little. Turn it off immediately and place the uncovered pan in the oven. Leave the pan in the oven for 1½ hours, until the dough is puffy and the slices fill the pan almost completely.

Remove the pan and preheat the oven to 350°.

6. Bake the pull-aparts for one hour. Remove them from the oven and let them cool in the pan on a wire rack for exactly five minutes. Cover the pan tightly with an inverted serving platter and turn the platter and pan over. The pull-aparts should drop onto the serving platter within a few seconds; if they don't, hold the platter and pan together, lift and tap them lightly on the counter or table. The pull-aparts should now drop from the pan onto the platter.

Let the pull-aparts cool slightly and then serve warm with butter.

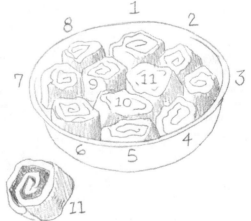

CINNAMON PRUNE YOGURT CAKE

MAKES ONE 9-INCH RING

This recipe makes a handsome, spicy ring cake, studded with chunks of prune. The yogurt adds a wonderful flavor, although the cake doesn't taste at all like yogurt.

BAKING PAN: ONE 9-INCH FLUTED TUBE PAN, 3¾ INCHES DEEP

PAN PREPARATION: GREASE AND FLOUR

PREHEAT OVEN TO 350°

BAKING TIME: ONE HOUR

30 whole pitted prunes
2 cups flour
2 teaspoons baking powder
½ teaspoon salt
1 teaspoon cinnamon
1 cup (one 8-ounce container)
  unflavored yogurt

1 scant teaspoon baking soda
½ cup (1 stick) butter, softened
1¼ cups sugar
2 eggs, separated
1 teaspoon vanilla extract

1. Cut each pitted prune in quarters and set aside.

Stir or whisk together the flour, baking powder, salt and cinnamon; set aside. In another bowl, stir together the yogurt and baking soda; the mixture will bubble and foam. Set aside.

2. In a large bowl, cream the butter and sugar until light. Add the egg yolks and vanilla and beat well.

3. Add the the dry ingredients and the yogurt mixture alternately, in three parts each, blending well after each addition. Stir in the prune pieces.

4. In another bowl, with clean, dry beaters, beat the egg whites until they stand in firm, glossy, moist peaks. Fold the egg whites into the batter. Pour the batter into the prepared pan, spreading it evenly.

5. Bake for one hour or until a cake tester inserted in the center of the cake comes out clean. Let the cake cool in the pan on a wire rack for five minutes and then turn it out to finish cooling rounded side up on the rack.

PEACH AND BLUEBERRY KUCHEN

MAKES ONE 9-INCH ROUND CAKE

A simple layer topped with sliced fresh peaches and lots of blueberries. The cake is mildly sweet and the fruit is juicy, perfect for breakfast or a mid-morning snack. The texture of this cake is especially nice.

TIP: To turn this into a dessert cake, top each wedge with a spoonful of sweetened whipped cream.

BAKING PAN: ONE 9-INCH SPRINGFORM PAN
PAN PREPARATION: GREASE
PREHEAT OVEN TO 350°
BAKING TIME: 45 MINUTES

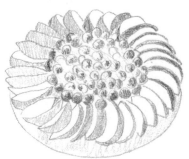

4 medium-size ripe peaches
½ fresh lemon
¾ cup fresh blueberries
1½ cups flour
2 teaspoons baking powder
¼ teaspoon salt
1 egg
½ cup sugar
⅓ cup milk

¼ cup (½ stick) butter,
　melted and cooled
½ teaspoon vanilla extract
¼ cup confectioners' sugar

1. Prepare the fruit: Peel the peaches by immersing them for one minute in a pot of simmering water. Remove the peaches from the hot water and run under cold water until cool enough to handle. The skins will slip off easily. Cut each peach in half and remove the pit. Cut in quarters and pare away any hard matter clinging to the centers. Cut each quarter in half so you have eight slices from each peach. Put the slices in a bowl, squeeze the lemon over them and toss to coat; this will keep them from turning brown.

Pick over the blueberries and discard any stems, leaves and moldy or mushy berries; if necessary, add more berries to measure ¾ cup. Rinse the berries and spread them on a paper towel to dry. Set the fruit aside.

2. Stir or whisk together the flour, baking powder and salt; set aside.

3. In a large bowl, beat the egg. Add the sugar, milk, melted butter and vanilla and beat until well blended.

4. Stir the dry ingredients into the egg mixture, blending just until moistened.

5. Spread the batter evenly in the prepared pan. Arrange the sliced peaches on the batter to make a border and put the blueberries in the center, as shown in the

drawing at the beginning of the recipe. Press the fruit lightly into the batter. Use a fine strainer to sift the confectioners' sugar over the fruit.

   6. Bake for 45 minutes; the cake will be pulling away from the sides of the pan. (Do not test with a cake tester because you will not get a reliable result; if your oven temperature is accurate, 45 minutes will be the right amount of baking time.) The confectioners' sugar will be transparent over the peaches and white on the blueberries.

   Let the cake cool in the pan on a wire rack for ten minutes. Release and remove the sides of the pan and let the cake finish cooling on the rack.

CHAPTER 6

Cakes with Fresh Fruit

STRAWBERRY SHORTCAKE
RASPBERRIES-AND-CREAM CAKE
BLUEBERRY BUTTERMILK SPICE SQUARES
CRANBERRY-FILLED LEMON LOAF
WALNUT GINGER PEAR TORTE
CARAMELIZED APPLE CAKE
QUICK PLUM CAKE

When making the cakes in this chapter, try to take advantage of whatever fine seasonal fruits your local farms have to offer—put Strawberry Shortcake or Raspberries-and-Cream Cake on the menu if you find locally grown berries in your produce market.

If you can't get locally grown fruit, buy the best seasonal fresh fruit available. Always choose ripe fruit (with the exception of the unripe pears needed for the Walnut Ginger Pear Torte) and be sure it has no bruises, mold or other blemishes. Frozen fruit is not an acceptable substitute in these recipes.

STRAWBERRY SHORTCAKE

MAKES TEN SMALL CAKES

What's the right way to make classic American strawberry shortcake? There is no one right way, but this traditional version using a rich biscuit dough is delicious.

BAKING PAN: ONE COOKIE SHEET
PAN PREPARATION: NONE
PREHEAT OVEN TO 450°
BAKING TIME: 12 MINUTES

For the filling and topping:
30 medium-large strawberries
½ cup sugar
1½ cups heavy cream, very cold
3–4½ tablespoons confectioners' sugar
2 teaspoons vanilla extract

For the shortcake:
2 cups flour
¼ cup sugar
3 teaspoons baking powder
½ teaspoon salt
6 tablespoons cold butter
⅓ cup milk
⅓ cup sour cream
   NOTE: If necessary, use ⅔ cup milk and eliminate the sour cream.
Melted butter

1. Rinse, drain, dry and hull the berries. Pick out 15 perfect berries of approximately equal size. Cut each perfect berry in half and set the halves aside for topping the cakes (step 6).

Cut the remaining 15 berries in ¼-inch slices. Mix them in a bowl with the ½ cup of sugar, crushing them slightly. Set aside for one hour or until serving time, stirring occasionally (see step 5).

2. Make the shortcake dough in a food processor with a steel chopping blade or by hand.

In a food processor: Put the flour, sugar, baking powder and salt in the bowl of the processor and mix with a few bursts of power. Add the butter in chunks and process just until the mixture looks like fine crumbs or cornmeal. In a separate bowl, stir the milk and sour cream together and add to the processor bowl. Process just until the dough forms one or two balls that sit on top of the steel blade.

By hand: Put the flour, sugar, baking powder and salt in a large bowl and stir. Using a pastry blender, cut the butter into the dry ingredients until the mixture looks like fine crumbs or cornmeal. Stir the milk and sour cream together in a small bowl, add to the butter mixture and blend just until you can form a ball of dough.

3. Turn the dough out onto a floured surface and knead lightly for 20 strokes.

Pat or roll the dough out to a thickness of ¾ inch and cut with a 2½-inch round biscuit cutter to make ten cakes (there will be some dough left over). Place the cakes on the cookie sheet, leaving two inches between them. Brush the tops with a little melted butter.

4. Bake for 12 minutes, until the tops are light gold; the bottoms will be brown. Watch carefully and do not overbake. Transfer the cakes to a wire rack to cool.

5. Just before serving, drain and reserve the juice from the bowl of sliced berries. In a large bowl, whip the heavy cream, confectioners' sugar and vanilla together until slightly stiffer than soft peaks. Do not overbeat.

6. With a fork, split one cake in half and brush the split sides with some of the reserved strawberry juice. Place the bottom half split side up on a large serving platter or an individual dessert plate and top it with a dollop of whipped cream, a spoonful of sliced berries and another dollop of whipped cream. Cover with the top half, split side down. Brush juice on the top. Add a dollop of whipped cream and three of the reserved strawberry halves. Drizzle a little strawberry juice over the top.

Repeat to make the rest of the short-cakes. Serve as soon as possible.

TIP: At first these strawberry short-cakes tend to lean and even topple, so keep an eye on them until they settle.

RASPBERRIES-AND-CREAM CAKE

MAKES ONE 9-INCH ROUND CAKE

Here is a butter sponge layer cake gently flavored with fresh raspberry purée, filled with sweetened whipped cream and crushed berries and decorated with plump whole berries. It's one of the best summer cakes I've ever tasted—light, delicate and rich at the same time.

TIP: Best on the day it is made but quite good on the second day, too; keep it refrigerated and serve it well chilled.

BAKING PAN: TWO 9-INCH ROUND CAKE PANS

PAN PREPARATION: GREASE; LINE EACH PAN WITH A WAXED PAPER CIRCLE; GREASE THE WAXED PAPER CIRCLES; DUST THE PANS WITH FLOUR

PREHEAT OVEN TO 350°

BAKING TIME: 25–30 MINUTES

1 pint box of fresh raspberries (about two cups)
3 tablespoons sugar
Ingredients for Butter Sponge Layer Cake (page 34)
2 cups heavy cream, very cold

1. Rinse the berries gently and put them on paper towels to air-dry. Set aside ½ cup of the prettiest whole berries for decorating the top of the cake.

Put ¾ cup of the remaining whole berries in a small bowl and mash them lightly with two teaspoons of the sugar, breaking up all the berries; set aside.

Put the remaining ¾ cup of berries in a small saucepan and stir with one teaspoon of the remaining sugar. Cook over low heat for a few minutes, mashing well, to make a purée. Let the purée cool completely.

2. Make the batter for Butter Sponge Layer Cake (page 34). Gently fold the cooled raspberry purée into the batter. Pour the batter into the prepared pans and bake as described in the recipe.

3. When the cake layers are completely cool, split each layer to make a total of four layers (how-to, page 20).

4. In a large bowl, whip the heavy cream with the remaining two tablespoons of sugar, beating until stiff. Stir in the mashed berries.

Put the bottom half of one layer on a serving platter and spread with one cup of the whipped cream filling. Repeat with the other three layers, ending with the top half of a layer and all of the remaining whipped cream.

Decorate the top of the cake with the reserved whole berries.

BLUEBERRY BUTTERMILK SPICE SQUARES

MAKES 24 SQUARES

This cake has a mild spice flavor and is terrifically moist and tender. If the combination of fresh blueberries and spice is new to you, you'll be delighted with the discovery. The cake is delicious warm or cool, plain or with slightly sweetened whipped cream or a scoop of ice cream.

BAKING PAN: ONE 9 × 13 × 2-INCH SHEET CAKE PAN

PAN PREPARATION: GREASE AND FLOUR

PREHEAT OVEN TO 350°

BAKING TIME: 40–45 MINUTES

2 cups fresh blueberries
1¾ cups flour
1 teaspoon baking powder
1 teaspoon baking soda
¼ teaspoon salt
½ teaspoon cinnamon
⅛ teaspoon ground cloves

⅛ teaspoon ground ginger
¾ cup (1½ sticks) butter, softened
½ cup sugar
½ cup light brown sugar
2 eggs, beaten
¾ cup buttermilk

1. Pick over the blueberries and discard any stems, leaves and moldy or unripe berries. Rinse the berries and spread them out on paper towels to air-dry; set aside.

Stir or whisk together the flour, baking powder, baking soda, salt and spices; set aside.

2. In a large bowl, cream the butter until light. Add the white and brown sugars gradually, beating well after each addition.

3. Pour in the beaten eggs a little at a time, beating well after each addition. When all the eggs are incorporated, beat for another two minutes at medium speed.

4. Add the dry ingredients and the buttermilk alternately, in three parts each, beating well after each addition.

5. Stir in the blueberries, being careful not to puncture them. Pour the batter into the prepared pan and spread evenly with a spatula.

6. Bake for 40–45 minutes or until the top is golden brown and a cake tester inserted in the center of the cake comes out free of batter. Do not overbake.

Let the cake cool in the pan on a wire rack and serve squares right from the pan.

CRANBERRY-FILLED LEMON LOAF

MAKES ONE LOAF

Ruby red pockets of tart cranberry filling enhance this moist lemon tea cake.

BAKING PAN: ONE 9½ × 5½ × 2¾-INCH LOAF PAN
PAN PREPARATION: GREASE AND FLOUR
PREHEAT OVEN TO 350°
BAKING TIME: 55–60 MINUTES

For the filling:
1½ cups fresh cranberries
½ cup sugar
1 tablespoon grated lemon rind
1 tablespoon cranberry juice,
    orange juice or water

For the batter:
2 cups flour
2 teaspoons baking powder
½ teaspoon baking soda
¼ teaspoon salt
¾ cup sugar
1 egg
⅔ cup milk
3 tablespoons butter, melted and
    cooled
3 tablespoons fresh lemon juice
½ teaspoon vanilla extract

1. Make the filling: In a food processor or blender, grind the cranberries, sugar, lemon rind and liquid to make a purée. Transfer the purée to a small saucepan and cook it over very low heat for 15 minutes, stirring often, until it is thickened and not runny. Set aside to cool.

2. In a large bowl, stir or whisk together the flour, baking powder, baking soda, salt and sugar; set aside.

3. In another bowl, whisk together the egg, milk, melted butter, lemon juice and vanilla. Add the egg mixture to the dry ingredients and beat just until all the ingredients are moistened.

4. Spoon half of the batter into the prepared pan and spread it evenly. Dot the batter with small mounds of filling, using about half of the purée.

Spoon the rest of the batter over the filling, spread it evenly and dot with small mounds of the remaining filling. Pull a knife back and forth through the batter and filling once, to marble it.

5. Bake for 55–60 minutes or until the cake is brown on top and a cake tester inserted in the center of the cake comes out free of batter.

Let the cake cool in the pan on a wire rack for ten minutes. Turn out and let it finish cooling right side up on the rack.

WALNUT GINGER PEAR TORTE

MAKES ONE 9-INCH CAKE

Tortes are often made without flour, as this one is; bread crumbs, chopped nuts and ground nuts are used instead. This torte also includes both chopped and sliced pears. Be sure the pears are *not* ripe; juicy, ripe pears will exude too much liquid and make the torte soggy.

BAKING PAN: ONE 9-INCH SPRINGFORM PAN
PAN PREPARATION: GREASE AND FLOUR
PREHEAT OVEN TO 350°
BAKING TIME: 75 MINUTES

5 unripe Comice or Anjou pears
1¼ cups sugar
½ teaspoon ground ginger
Squeeze of fresh lemon juice
1 cup lightly packed fresh white
  bread crumbs (no crusts)
½ cup finely chopped walnuts
½ cup ground walnuts
1 teaspoon baking powder
1 teaspoon grated lemon rind
Pinch of salt

4 eggs, separated
1 teaspoon vanilla extract

For the decoration and topping
  (optional):
Crystallized ginger, slivered
Basic Sweetened Whipped Cream
  (page 168)

1. Peel three of the pears and quarter them lengthwise. Core each quarter carefully, removing all the hard matter from the center, and chop the quarters into ½-inch-wide pieces. Put the chopped pears in a saucepan with ½ cup of the sugar, the ginger and lemon juice. Cook uncovered over low heat for a few minutes, stirring often, until the pears are just beginning to soften. Drain the pears and set them aside to cool. Return the syrup to the saucepan and set it aside.

Stir together the bread crumbs, walnuts, baking powder, lemon rind and salt; set aside.

2. Put the egg yolks and ½ cup of the remaining sugar in a large bowl and beat at medium speed for three to five minutes, until very thick and pale. Add the vanilla and beat again to blend.

3. Stir the dry ingredients and the cooked pears into the egg yolk mixture.

4. In another large bowl, with clean, dry beaters, beat the egg whites until frothy. Add the remaining ¼ cup of sugar and beat the egg whites until they stand in firm, glossy, moist peaks. Fold a third of the egg whites into the batter to lighten it; fold the rest of the egg whites into the lightened batter.

Pour the batter into the springform pan and spread it evenly.

5. Peel the two remaining pears and quarter them lengthwise. Core each quarter carefully and then cut each quarter lengthwise into three slices, for a total of 24 slices. Arrange the slices on top of the batter as shown in the drawing at the beginning of the recipe.

6. Bake the torte at 350° for one hour. Meanwhile, cook the reserved syrup over low heat until it is thickened but still runny and reduced by about half. When the torte has baked for one hour at 350°, open the oven and baste the sliced pears with the syrup. Reduce the oven temperature to 325° and bake for 15 minutes more.

Remove the torte from the oven and immediately run a sharp knife around it to loosen it from the sides of the pan. Let the torte cool in the pan on a wire rack for ten minutes and then release and remove the sides of the pan. Brush the top of the torte with more warm syrup and let it cool completely on the rack.

Leave the torte on the bottom of the pan and place it on a serving platter. If you like, sprinkle the top of the torte with slivers of crystallized ginger and serve with a bowl of sweetened whipped cream.

CARAMELIZED APPLE CAKE

MAKES ONE 9-INCH ROUND CAKE

This is one of my favorite autumn cakes—really rich and buttery, with the incomparable flavor of caramelized sugar. It is basically an upside-down cake, very easy to make.

TIP: The recipe calls for *tart* apples; don't substitute sweet ones because you do need the contrast between the sweet syrup and tart fruit.

BAKING PAN: ONE 9-INCH ROUND OR OVAL FLAMEPROOF, OVENPROOF CASSEROLE, TWO TO THREE INCHES DEEP (SEE NOTE BEFORE STEP 1)

PAN PREPARATION: SEE STEP 2

PREHEAT OVEN TO 425°

BAKING TIME: 20 MINUTES

For the caramelized apples:
6 medium-size tart apples
½ cup (1 stick) butter
1¼ cups sugar

For the batter:
1½ cups flour
¾ cup sugar
2 teaspoons baking powder
½ teaspoon salt
2 eggs
2 tablespoons butter, melted and cooled
6 tablespoons milk
1 teaspoon vanilla extract

NOTE: The casserole dish may be ceramic, enameled cast iron, stainless steel or another material but it *must* be a dish that can be subjected to both direct (stove-top) heat and radiant (oven) heat.

1. Prepare the apples: Peel the apples and cut them in quarters. Core them carefully, making sure you remove all the seeds and other hard matter in the center of each piece. Rinse and then pat dry with paper towels.

2. Caramelize the apples: Melt the half cup of butter in the casserole over low heat, brushing some butter up the sides of the casserole. Add the 1¼ cups sugar and stir until the sugar is moistened. Turn off the heat while you arrange the apples on the sugar with cored sides up as shown, overlapping and wedging the pieces together to fit. Use all 24 pieces of apple.

Turn the heat back on to low and continue cooking for about 20 minutes, until the sugar dissolves completely and caramelizes to a pale amber. During the cooking, press the apples down occasionally and spoon sugar syrup over them, without disturbing the arrangement.

Remove from the heat and set aside while you make the batter.

3. Stir or whisk together the flour, sugar, baking powder and salt; set aside.

In a large bowl, whisk together the eggs, melted butter, milk and vanilla. Add the flour mixture and stir just until blended.

Cover the apples carefully with an even layer of batter, dropping the batter by tablespoonsful onto the apples, using up all the batter. Again, try not to disturb the arrangement of apples.

4. Bake for 20 minutes or until the top is lightly browned and a cake tester inserted in the center of the cake (not in the apples) comes out clean. Remove the casserole from the oven and let it rest on a wire rack for five minutes.

Cover the casserole tightly with an inverted serving platter and flip the casserole and platter to turn out the cake. Carefully remove the casserole and let the cake cool on the platter. One or two apple slices may slide off the cake—simply press them in place with a spoon and they will stick as the cake cools. Use a pastry brush to scoop up and paint onto the cake any syrup that collects on the serving platter.

Serve warm or cool, with unsweetened whipped cream if you like.

QUICK PLUM CAKE

MAKES ONE 8-INCH SQUARE CAKE

I have been baking this cake for many years. It's one of my standbys because it is quick and simple to make and tastes luxurious even though the ingredients are rather humble. Also, the recipe can easily be doubled and made in a 9 × 13 × 2-inch sheet cake pan; use 18 prune-plums arranged as shown in the drawing following step 4.

BAKING PAN: ONE 8-INCH SQUARE CAKE PAN (BROWNIE PAN)

PAN PREPARATION: GREASE

PREHEAT OVEN TO 375°

BAKING TIME: 40 MINUTES

10 Italian prune-plums (small oval plums)
1½ cups flour
2 teaspoons baking powder
½ teaspoon salt
1 cup plus two tablespoons sugar
½ cup cold margarine

1 egg
½ cup milk
1 teaspoon vanilla extract
½ teaspoon cinnamon
2 tablespoons butter, melted and cooled

1. Cut each plum in half lengthwise and discard the pits. Set aside the plum halves.

2. In a large bowl, stir or whisk together the flour, baking powder, salt and ten tablespoons of the sugar. Cut the margarine into pats and use a pastry blender to work the margarine into the dry ingredients until the mixture looks like crumbs.

NOTE: This step is easy to do in a food processor. Put the dry ingredients in the bowl of the processor and mix with a few bursts of power. Add the pats of margarine and process for another few seconds until the mixture looks like crumbs. Transfer the mixture to a large bowl.

3. Add the egg, milk and vanilla and blend with a fork just until the flour mixture is moistened. Spoon the batter into the prepared pan and spread it evenly.

4. Arrange the plum halves *skin side up* in neat rows on the batter. Push each plum down into the batter slightly, so it is firmly embedded.

5. Mix together the remaining ½ cup of sugar and the cinnamon and sprinkle evenly over the plums and batter. (This will seem like a lot of sugar, since it will almost completely cover the plums. However, it is the correct amount.) Drizzle the melted butter evenly over the cinnamon sugar.

6. Bake for 40 minutes or until a cake tester inserted in the center of the cake comes out clean. Let the cake cool in the pan on a wire rack.

Serve squares of cake warm or cool, right from the pan.

OTHER CAKES MADE WITH FRESH FRUIT:

Strawberry-Crowned Devil's Food Cake with Sour Cream Frosting,
    page 54
Peach and Blueberry Kuchen, page 83
Banana Layer Cake, page 99
Applesauce Stack Cake, page 106

CHAPTER 7

Favorite Traditional Cakes

MISSISSIPPI MUD CAKE

BANANA LAYER CAKE

OLD-FASHIONED JAM ROLL

SOUTHERN BOURBON PECAN CAKE

PINEAPPLE UPSIDE-DOWN CAKE

NEW YORK CHEESECAKE

APPLESAUCE STACK CAKE

FRESH COCONUT LAYER CAKE

It has always seemed to me that American cake-lovers are especially lucky because we are the heirs to a remarkable variety of baking recipes and traditions. American home bakers have preserved and adapted so many wonderful recipes from so many different countries, invented hundreds more—and somehow managed to infuse them all with a distinctively American flavor and style.

No cookbook can include every one of the best cake recipes, but this chapter offers a sampling of delicious national and regional favorites. Perhaps you will find here a recipe that helps re-create the taste of your own best-loved traditional cake.

MISSISSIPPI MUD CAKE

MAKES ONE 9-INCH ROUND CAKE

This triple-chocolate cake (made with cocoa, semisweet chocolate and chocolate chips) sends chocolate fans into swoons. It is cake-like around the edges, soft and fudgy in the center and so rich that a small piece goes a long way.

BAKING PAN: ONE 9-INCH SPRINGFORM PAN
PAN PREPARATION: GREASE AND FLOUR
PREHEAT OVEN TO 400°
BAKING TIME: 35 MINUTES

1 cup flour
¼ cup unsweetened cocoa powder
¼ teaspoon salt
1 cup butter, softened
9 tablespoons sugar
3 tablespoons safflower or corn oil

4 eggs, beaten
1 teaspoon vanilla extract
2½ tablespoons light corn syrup
8 ounces (8 squares) semisweet
    chocolate, melted and cooled
1 cup semisweet chocolate chips

1. Stir or whisk together the flour, cocoa powder and salt; set aside.

2. In a large bowl, cream the butter until light. Gradually add the sugar, beating well after each addition.

3. Add the oil and beat for 1½ minutes at medium speed, until the mixture is smooth.

4. Add the beaten eggs a little at a time, beating well after each addition. The mixture should be fluffy. Add the vanilla and corn syrup and beat at medium speed for three more minutes.

5. Beat in the melted chocolate.

6. Using a fine strainer, sift the dry ingredients over the batter a little at a time and fold well after each addition. Gently stir in the chocolate chips.

Pour and spoon the batter into the prepared pan and spread it evenly.

7. Bake for 35 minutes or until a cake tester inserted about half an inch from the edge of the cake comes out clean. (The center of the cake will be soft and sludgy, so don't insert the cake tester in the center.)

Let the cake cool for five minutes in the pan on a wire rack. Run a knife around the edge of the cake and then release and remove the sides of the springform pan. Leave the cake on the bottom of the pan and place on a serving platter.

Serve with unsweetened whipped cream.

BANANA LAYER CAKE

MAKES A TWO-LAYER ROUND CAKE

Here's a classic banana cake, lightly flavored with cinnamon and nutmeg, with a luscious pastry cream between the layers and on top of the cake. You have the option of stirring chopped walnuts into the batter to make it a Banana Walnut Layer Cake.

BAKING PAN: TWO 9-INCH ROUND CAKE PANS

PAN PREPARATION: GREASE AND FLOUR

PREHEAT OVEN TO 350°

BAKING TIME: 25 MINUTES

2 cups flour
2½ teaspoons baking powder
½ teaspoon baking soda
½ teaspoon salt
1 teaspoon cinnamon
½ teaspoon nutmeg
1 cup mashed ripe bananas (about three small bananas)
¼ cup sour cream
½ cup (1 stick) butter, softened
1 cup sugar

2 eggs, beaten
1 teaspoon vanilla extract
1 cup chopped walnuts (optional)

For the filling and frosting:
½ cup heavy cream, very cold
1¼ cups Basic Vanilla Pastry Cream (page 170)
Whole or chopped walnuts for decoration

1. Stir or whisk together the flour, baking powder, baking soda, salt and spices; set aside. Stir together the mashed bananas and sour cream; set aside.

2. In a large bowl, cream the butter until light. Gradually add the sugar, beating well after each addition.

3. Pour in the beaten eggs a little at a time, beating well after each addition. Continue beating for another two minutes at medium speed. Add the vanilla and the banana mixture and blend well.

4. Add the dry ingredients in six parts, blending well after each addition. If you are making Banana Walnut Layer Cake, stir the chopped walnuts into the batter now.

Spoon equal amounts of batter into the prepared pans and spread the batter evenly.

5. Bake for 25 minutes or until a cake tester inserted in the center of the cake comes out clean. Let the layers cool in the pans on wire racks for ten minutes, then turn them out to finish cooling right side up on the racks.

6. To fill and frost the cake, beat the heavy cream until stiff and fold it into the Basic Vanilla Pastry Cream. Place one cake layer on a serving platter and spread half the lightened pastry cream on it, not quite to the edges. Cover with the second layer and spread with the remaining pastry cream. Press chopped or whole walnuts on the top of the cake.

Refrigerate until half an hour before serving.

OLD-FASHIONED JAM ROLL

MAKES ONE ROLL ABOUT TEN INCHES LONG

Many good bakers shy away from rolled cakes because they have never been able to roll one without breaking it and making a mess. I promise you complete success if you follow this recipe carefully.

BAKING PAN: ONE 10½ × 15½ × 1-INCH JELLY ROLL PAN
PAN PREPARATION: GREASE; LINE COMPLETELY (BOTTOM AND SIDES) WITH WAXED PAPER; GREASE THE WAXED PAPER
PREHEAT OVEN TO 400°
BAKING TIME: 10–12 MINUTES

¾ **cup cake flour**
¾ **teaspoon baking powder**
¼ **teaspoon salt**
5 **eggs, room temperature, separated**

¾ **cup sugar**
1 **teaspoon vanilla extract**
¾ **cup good-quality, thick jam (see note before step 1)**
Confectioners' sugar

NOTE: Chunky preserves work well for the filling if they are puréed in a food processor or blender before measuring.

1. Sift together the cake flour, baking powder and salt; set aside.

2. In a large bowl, beat the egg yolks until thick and pale. Gradually add six tablespoons of the sugar, beating after each addition; the mixture should fall in a thick ribbon when the beaters are lifted. Add the vanilla and beat again.

3. In another large bowl, with clean, dry beaters, beat the egg whites until foamy. Gradually add the remaining sugar, beating constantly, until the whites stand in firm, glossy, moist peaks. Fold a third of the egg whites into the yolk mixture to lighten it; fold the rest of the egg whites into the lightened yolk mixture.

4. Using a fine strainer, gradually sift the dry ingredients into the egg mixture, folding them in gently but thoroughly. Spread the batter evenly in the prepared pan, especially into the corners. Put it in the oven immediately.

5. Bake for 10–12 minutes or just until the cake is golden on top and a cake tester inserted in the center comes out clean. Do not overbake.

While the cake is baking, get out a clean linen or other lint-free dish towel and a wire rack or cookie sheet larger than the jelly roll pan.

When the cake is done, remove the pan from the oven. Working quickly, cover the pan first with the towel and then with the *inverted* wire rack or cookie sheet. Flip the pan, towel and rack to turn out the cake. Remove the pan and then carefully and slowly peel off the waxed paper.

Slide the towel and cake onto the table or counter; the cake is wrong side up. Cut off any crisp edges. Fold one end of the towel over the short end of the cake and roll up the cake in the towel.

Place the rolled cake seam side down on the wire rack to cool.

6. When the cake is completely cool, unroll it, leaving it on the towel. You'll notice that the cake looks rather flattened; it will perk up in a few minutes. Spread the jam evenly over the cake, all the way to the edges.

Roll up the cake again, this time without the towel (but using the towel to help roll); a little of the cake may stick to the towel as you peel the towel away. Place the cake seam side down on a serving platter.

Tuck strips of waxed paper under the cake roll (how-to, page 24) and sift confectioners' sugar over it. Carefully pull away and discard the waxed paper strips. Cut a thin slice off each end of the jam roll to neaten it up.

Serve plain or with whipped cream, ice cream or sherbet.

NOTE: Old-Fashioned Jam Roll need not be filled with jam—you can fill it with buttercream frosting or pastry cream (Chapter 11), softened ice cream or Homemade Applesauce (page 107). And instead of confectioners' sugar, try topping the roll with glaze or flavored whipped cream (Chapter 11).

step 5

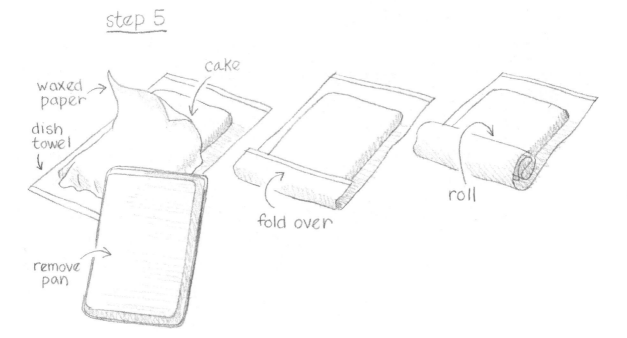

waxed paper

cake

dish towel

remove pan

fold over

roll

SOUTHERN BOURBON PECAN CAKE

MAKES ONE 10½-INCH TUBE CAKE

A dense, almost chewy cake with a distinct bourbon taste, good for holiday parties since it is both large and rich. And you don't have to be southern to love it.

BAKING PAN: 10½-INCH TUBE PAN, THREE INCHES DEEP
PAN PREPARATION: GREASE AND FLOUR
PREHEAT OVEN TO 325°
BAKING TIME: ONE HOUR

3 cups flour
1 teaspoon baking powder
½ teaspoon baking soda
½ teaspoon salt
½ teaspoon nutmeg
1 cup sugar
1¼ cups light brown sugar

⅔ cup bourbon whiskey
½ cup orange marmalade, puréed
   in blender or food processor
1 cup (2 sticks) butter, softened
4 eggs
2½–3 cups coarsely chopped pecans

1. Stir or whisk together the flour, baking powder, baking soda, salt and nutmeg; set aside. In another bowl, stir together the white and light brown sugars and set aside. In a third bowl, stir together the bourbon and puréed marmalade and set aside.

2. Cream the butter until light. Gradually add half the sugar mixture, beating well after each addition.

3. In a separate bowl, beat the eggs for several minutes at high speed, until they are very pale, frothy and quadrupled in volume. Gradually add the remaining sugar mixture, beating well after each addition. The egg mixture should be thick and billowy.

4. Pour the egg mixture into the butter mixture and beat well at high speed. Add the dry ingredients and the bourbon mixture alternately, in three parts each, beating well after each addition.

5. Stir the chopped pecans into the batter. Pour and spoon the batter into the prepared pan and spread the batter evenly.

6. Bake for one hour or until a cake tester inserted in the center of the cake comes out clean. Let the cake cool in the pan on a wire rack for 15 minutes and then turn the cake out to finish cooling rounded side up on the rack.

PINEAPPLE UPSIDE-DOWN CAKE

MAKES ONE 9-INCH ROUND CAKE

I generally prefer cakes made with fresh fruit rather than canned fruit (see Chapter 6), but Pineapple Upside-Down Cake is the exception to the rule. In fact, I keep a can of pineapple slices in the pantry so that I can make this familiar and comforting cake whenever I need a reminder of the past.

BAKING PAN: ONE 9-INCH ROUND CAKE PAN

PAN PREPARATION: SEE STEP 1

PREHEAT OVEN TO 400°

BAKING TIME: 30 MINUTES

¾ cup (1½ sticks) butter, melted and cooled
¾ cup dark brown sugar
7 pineapple slices (from a 20-ounce can)
¼ cup pineapple juice (reserved from the can of pineapple)

1½ cups flour
2 teaspoons baking powder
½ teaspoon salt
½ cup sugar
½ cup milk
1 egg
½ teaspoon vanilla extract

1. Put four tablespoons of the melted butter in the cake pan and tilt the pan back and forth to coat the bottom. Brush a little melted butter up the sides of the pan.

Sprinkle the brown sugar evenly over the melted butter. Arrange the pineapple slices on the brown sugar as shown in the drawing and sprinkle the rings with the pineapple juice; set the cake pan aside.

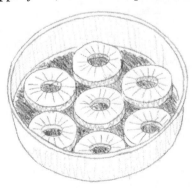

2. In a large bowl, stir or whisk together the flour, baking powder, salt and white sugar.

3. Add the milk, egg, vanilla and the remaining melted butter and beat just until the batter is blended and smooth. Carefully spoon the batter over the pineapple slices in the pan.

4. Bake for 30 minutes or until a cake tester inserted in the cake (not in the pineapple) comes out clean.

Let the cake cool in the pan on a wire rack for ten minutes. Cover the pan tightly with an inverted serving platter and flip the pan and platter to turn out the cake pineapple side up.

Serve warm or cool. If you like, add dollops of unsweetened or lightly sweetened whipped cream.

NEW YORK CHEESECAKE

MAKES ONE 9-INCH CAKE

Real New York Cheesecake is smooth and light, not too fluffy (but not too dense, either), made with both cream cheese and sour cream. The crust is a classic combination of graham cracker crumbs and ground walnuts.

TIP: Follow the pan preparation and baking instructions carefully to produce a perfect cake with no major cracks marring the surface. (Don't let a few small cracks worry you.)

Thanks to Ruth Abrams for her contribution to the development of this recipe.

BAKING PAN: ONE 9-INCH SPRINGFORM PAN

PAN PREPARATION: SEE STEP 1

PREHEAT OVEN TO 350°

BAKING TIME: ONE HOUR; TOTAL OF THREE HOURS IN THE OVEN

For the crust:
1 cup honey graham cracker
   crumbs (about 7 whole crackers)
¼ cup ground walnuts
½ cup (1 stick) butter, melted and
   cooled
1 teaspoon sugar
Pinch of salt

For the filling:
1 pound (two 8-ounce packages)
   cream cheese, softened
1 cup (one 8-ounce container) sour
   cream
1 cup sugar
4 eggs, separated
1 teaspoon vanilla extract
3 tablespoons flour

1. Prepare the springform pan: Cut four pieces of aluminum foil, each 16 inches long. Stack them, centered, in different directions as shown in the drawing. Put the springform pan in the center of the stack and press the foil tightly up around the pan, folding the corners of the foil down even with the rim of the pan. Be careful not to puncture the foil, since this aluminum foil jacket will protect the contents of the pan when you place the pan in a water bath for baking.

Grease the pan.

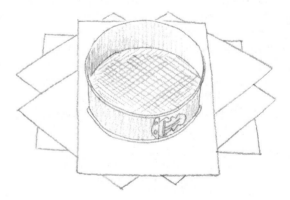

2. Make the crust: Stir the crust ingredients together. Put the mixture in the prepared springform pan and pat evenly over the bottom of the pan. Set the pan in the refrigerator.

3. Put the softened cream cheese in a large bowl and beat until it is light and smooth. Add the sour cream and beat again until smooth.

4. Blend in the sugar, then add the egg yolks and vanilla and beat again. Sprinkle the flour over the mixture and blend it in.

5. Fill a kettle with water and bring it to a boil.

Meanwhile, finish making the filling: In another large bowl, with clean, dry beaters, beat the egg whites until they hold firm, glossy, moist peaks. Fold them gently but thoroughly into the cream cheese mixture. Carefully pour the filling over the crust in the pan.

Place the filled springform pan in a larger pan (for instance, a broiler pan) on the center rack of the oven. Fill the larger pan with boiling water to a depth of one inch. Be careful not to get any water in the springform pan.

6. Bake the cheesecake for one hour and then turn off the oven. *Do not take the cheesecake out of the oven.* Prop the oven door open just a little, using the handle of a wooden spoon, and leave the cheesecake in the slowly cooling oven for two more hours. During that time, the cake will finish baking and will set properly.

At the end of the two hours, open the oven door and feel the top of the cake; it should be dry and just warm, not hot. (If the top of the cake is still hot, leave the cake in the oven for another hour.) Remove both pans from the oven.

Lift the springform pan out of the water bath and remove the aluminum foil jacket. If necessary, run a knife around the sides of the cake to loosen it from the pan; release and remove the sides of the pan. Leave the cheesecake on the bottom of the pan and place it on a wire rack to finish cooling completely.

Leaving the cheesecake on the bottom of the pan, put it in the refrigerator. When the cake is cold, run a long metal spatula under the crust to loosen it from the bottom of the pan; slide the cake onto a platter and return it to the refrigerator. Let it come to room temperature before serving.

top browns deeply
probably cooked at too high a temp
try 325 also could be baked in an 8" pan
Crust <u>very</u> nice

APPLESAUCE STACK CAKE

MAKES ONE FOUR-LAYER CAKE

Molasses-flavored Applesauce Stack Cake is actually baked as one square layer that is cut and split to make four thin layers. The layers are filled with Homemade Applesauce, which can be made at your convenience several days before you bake the cake.

BAKING PAN: ONE 9-INCH SQUARE CAKE PAN
PAN PREPARATION: GREASE AND FLOUR
PREHEAT OVEN TO 350°
BAKING TIME: 20 MINUTES

1¾ cups flour
1 teaspoon baking powder
¼ teaspoon baking soda
½ teaspoon salt
6 tablespoons butter, softened
¾ cup sugar
¼ cup unsulphured molasses
2 eggs, beaten
½ cup milk

Homemade Applesauce (recipe follows on page 107)
Vanilla Glaze (page 172)
Raisins or chopped walnuts (optional)

1. Stir or whisk together the flour, baking powder, baking soda and salt; set aside.

2. In a large bowl, cream the butter until light. Gradually add the sugar, beating well after each addition. Add the molasses and beat again.

3. Pour in the beaten eggs a little at a time, beating well after each addition.

4. Add the dry ingredients and the milk alternately, in three parts each, blending well after each addition. Pour the batter into the prepared pan.

5. Bake for 20 minutes or until a cake tester inserted in the center of the cake comes out clean. Let the cake cool in the pan on a wire rack for ten minutes and then turn it out to finish cooling right side up on the wire rack.

6. When the cake is completely cool, cut a thin slice off each side. Cut the cake in half and then carefully split each half into two layers as shown.

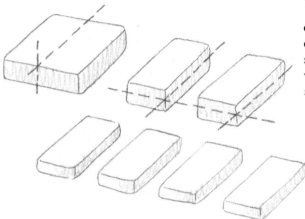

7. Put one bottom layer on a serving platter and tuck strips of waxed paper under it (how-to, page 24). Spread about ⅔ cup of Homemade Applesauce on the layer. Repeat with the rest of the layers and applesauce, ending with a top layer of cake (no applesauce on the top layer).

Thin the Vanilla Glaze with a little cream or milk. Pour and spread some glaze on top of the cake; while the glaze is still soft, you may press raisins or chopped walnuts into it. Remove the waxed paper strips and serve.

HOMEMADE APPLESAUCE

MAKES ABOUT 2 CUPS

6 large McIntosh apples
¼ cup dark brown sugar
½ cup applejack

2 tablespoons butter
Pinch of salt

1. Peel the apples and cut them in quarters. Carefully pare away all the seeds and hard matter from the center of each quarter. Cut each quarter in half.

2. Put all the ingredients in a heavy saucepan. Cover the pan and cook over low heat, stirring occasionally, until the apples fall apart. Help the process along by cutting up the apples with the edge of a spoon.

3. When the apples are mushy, uncover the pan and reduce the heat as much as possible. There will be a lot of liquid in the pan. Cook down the mixture, stirring often to prevent burning and mashing with the back of the spoon to make a fairly smooth sauce. This can take an hour or longer.

When the sauce is very thick and brown, remove it from the heat and allow it to cool. Store in the refrigerator until needed.

NOTE: The applesauce may be made several days ahead.

FRESH COCONUT LAYER CAKE

MAKES A TWO-LAYER ROUND CAKE

A coconut cake made with packaged coconut just can't be compared to the same cake made with the freshly grated or chopped meat of a coconut. In this recipe, fresh coconut goes into the batter and onto the fluffy frosting. Instructions for preparing the coconut are in step 1.

BAKING PAN: TWO 8-INCH ROUND CAKE PANS
PAN PREPARATION: GREASE AND FLOUR
PREHEAT OVEN TO 350° AFTER HEATING THE COCONUT
BAKING TIME: 35 MINUTES

1 fresh coconut (see note before step 1)
2 cups cake flour
1½ teaspoons baking powder
½ teaspoon salt
½ cup (1 stick) butter, softened
1¼ cups sugar

4 eggs, separated
1½ teaspoons vanilla extract
1 teaspoon coconut extract
½ cup milk

3½ cups Snowdrift Frosting (page 166)

NOTE: A fresh coconut is the brown nut you buy in the supermarket. Shake it before you buy it—you should hear plenty of liquid sloshing around inside.

1. Prepare the fresh coconut: First hammer a screwdriver through each of the three "eyes" at the end of the coconut and shake out the liquid. Put the drained coconut in a 400° oven for 25 minutes.

Firmly tap the hot coconut all over with the flat side of the hammer. Wrap the coconut in an old dish towel or clean rag, place it on a very hard surface (like a concrete sidewalk) and smack it with the flat side of the hammer or a heavy mallet until the shell cracks open. Pull out the pieces of coconut meat.

Use a vegetable peeler or sharp paring knife to remove the brown skin. Rinse and dry the pieces of white coconut meat. Break or cut the meat in small chunks and grate in a rotary hand grater or chop very fine in a blender or food processor (using the steel blade); set aside.

2. Stir or whisk together the cake flour, baking powder and salt; set aside.

3. In a large bowl, cream the butter until light. Gradually add ¾ cup of the sugar, beating well after each addition.

4. Add the egg yolks one at a time, beating well after each addition. Add the vanilla and the coconut extract and blend well.

5. Add the dry ingredients alternately with the milk, in three parts each, beating well after each addition. Stir in ¾ cup of the grated or chopped coconut.

6. In another large bowl, with clean, dry beaters, beat the egg whites until foamy. Gradually add the remaining ½ cup of sugar, beating until the egg whites stand in firm, glossy, moist peaks. Fold one-third of the egg whites into the batter to lighten it; fold the rest of the egg whites into the lightened batter.

Pour equal amounts of batter into the prepared pans and spread evenly.

7. Bake at 350° for 35 minutes or until a cake tester inserted in the center of the cake comes out clean. The top of the cake will be light brown.

Let the cake cool in the pans on wire racks for ten minutes. Turn the layers out to finish cooling right side up on the racks.

8. Fill and frost the cake: First brush or trim off any crisp, brown crumbs from the layers. Place one layer on a serving platter, tuck strips of waxed paper under it (how-to, page 24) and spread with 1½ cups of Snowdrift Frosting. Cover with the second layer. Use the remaining two cups of Snowdrift Frosting to frost the top and sides of the cake. Pat as much of the remaining coconut as possible first around the sides and then on the top, pressing it in so that it adheres. Remove the waxed paper strips.

Serve as soon as possible, storing any leftovers in a cake preserver since Snowdrift Frosting cannot be refrigerated or frozen.

OTHER TRADITIONAL CAKES TO MAKE:

Burnt Sugar Layer Cake, page 44
Dark Sweet Date-Nut Loaf, page 67
Filled Vienna Braid, page 74

Honey Pecan Pull-Aparts, page 80
Strawberry Shortcake, page 86

CHAPTER 8

Birthday Cakes and How to Decorate Them

BIRTHDAY LAYER CAKES WITH DECORATIONS
BIRTHDAY SHEET CAKES WITH DECORATIONS
ICE CREAM LAYER CAKE WITH WHIPPED CREAM FROSTING
ICE CREAM CAKE ROLL WITH RICH CHOCOLATE SAUCE
FANCY FROSTED CUPCAKES FOR KIDS

Does anyone ever really outgrow the heady delight of birthday parties? The fun of presents and singing and balloons and streamers—and especially of birthday cake? Whether your favorite is a layer cake with creamy frosting and fancy decorations, an ice cream cake extravaganza covered with whipped cream or a fleet of fancy cupcakes, you'll find it in this chapter.

When preparing a birthday cake, make the kind of cake and frosting the guest of honor likes best and be sure to put his or her name on the cake.

abcd Eleanor

ABC JOHN

abcd Maggie

abcd Jane

ABC MARNIE

abcd Sarah

ABC GORDON

ABCD AMY

BIRTHDAY LAYER CAKES WITH DECORATIONS

Follow the 1-2-3 Plan below, using layer cake recipes from Chapter 2, frostings and fillings from Chapter 11 and the decorating suggestions illustrated below and on page 114 to put together sensational birthday layer cakes.

NOTE: Read the Decorating Primer, pages 25–30, before reproducing the decorations given here; use Decorating Frosting, page 30, for all decorative piping.

1-2-3 PLAN

1. From the lists below, select a cake and an appropriate filling and frosting.

2. From the drawings on the next page, choose a decoration. Assemble any special ingredients and tools you will need for the decoration.

3. Bake, fill and frost the cake. Using the drawing as a guide, apply the chosen decoration to the top of the cake. Add decorations to the sides of the cake if desired.

CHOOSE A CAKE

Here are some layer cake suggestions:
♦ Yellow Layer Cake, page 32: two 8-inch layers
♦ White Layer Cake, page 36: three 8-inch layers or two 9-inch layers
♦ Chocolate Layer Cake, page 40: three 8-inch layers or two 9-inch layers
♦ Lemon Layer Cake, page 42: two 8-inch layers
♦ Banana Layer Cake, page 99: two 9-inch layers

CHOOSE A FILLING AND FROSTING

You are always safe choosing the (delicious) basics, provided the frosting is compatible with the cake:
♦ Basic Vanilla Buttercream Frosting, page 162
♦ Lemon Buttercream Frosting, page 164
♦ Mocha Buttercream Frosting, page 163
♦ Snowdrift Frosting, page 166 (which may be tinted or colored if desired)
♦ Double Chocolate Frosting, page 167

CHOOSE A DECORATION

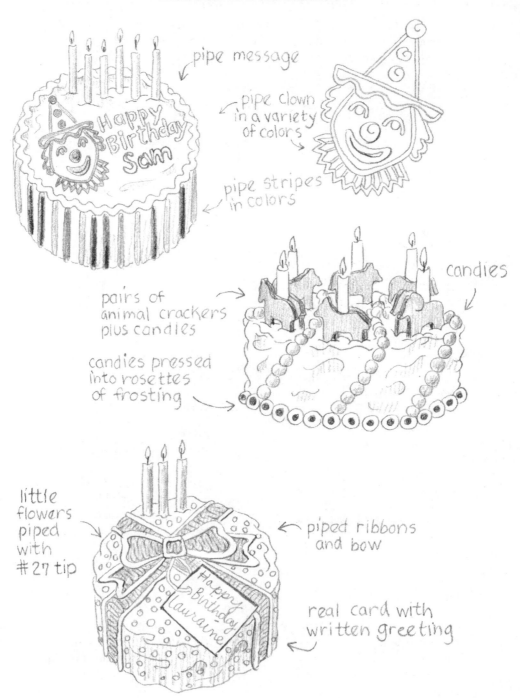

pipe message

pipe clown in a variety of colors

pipe stripes in colors

candies

pairs of animal crackers plus candies

candies pressed into rosettes of frosting

little flowers piped with #27 tip

piped ribbons and bow

real card with written greeting

Happy Birthday Sam

Happy Birthday Lauraine

BIRTHDAY SHEET CAKES WITH DECORATIONS

A sheet cake provides the space for you to create a theme decoration representing the hobby, profession or special interest of the birthday person. Follow the easy 1-2-3 Plan below.

NOTE: Read the Decorating Primer, pages 25–30, before frosting and decorating the cake. All the decorative piping is done with Decorating Frosting, page 30.

1-2-3 PLAN

1. From the lists below, select a sheet cake and a compatible frosting.

2. Look at the drawings on the next few pages and choose the decoration that best suits the birthday person *or* invent an appropriate design and make a sketch of it. Assemble the necessary ingredients and tools.

3. Make the sheet cake and carefully turn it out of the pan according to the recipe directions. Make the frosting (tint it, if you like) and frost the top and sides of the cake. Using one of the drawings here or your own sketch as a guide, create the decoration.

CHOOSE A CAKE

Here are some sheet cake suggestions:
◆ Sweet Cream Layer Cake or Sweet Cream Marble Cake, page 38
◆ Chocolate Layer Cake, page 40
◆ Lemon Layer Cake, page 42
◆ Burnt Sugar Layer Cake, page 44
◆ Best Carrot Cake Squares, page 69

CHOOSE A FROSTING

To make a tinted or brightly colored frosting, start with a light-colored one (how to tint and color, page 24):
◆ Basic Vanilla Buttercream Frosting, page 162
◆ Snowdrift Frosting, page 166
◆ Cream Cheese Frosting, page 169

These frostings are classics, sure to please everyone:
◆ Lemon or Orange Buttercream Frosting, page 164
◆ Mocha or Chocolate Buttercream Frosting, page 163
◆ Double Chocolate Frosting, page 167

CHOOSE A DECORATION

The decorating ideas shown on the following pages represent some popular pastimes. Reproduce them as shown or adapt the designs to suit the birthday person.

licorice stick & licorice string

piped fish, message, waves

candies

chocolate wafers

piping

piping

2 colors of frosting

Happy Birthday Gideon

HAPPY·BIRTHDAY BENJAMIN

piped lettering

HAPPY BIRTHDAY SUSAN

pipe bat & fill in with frosting

cut mitt from apricot leather, add piping

chopped nuts

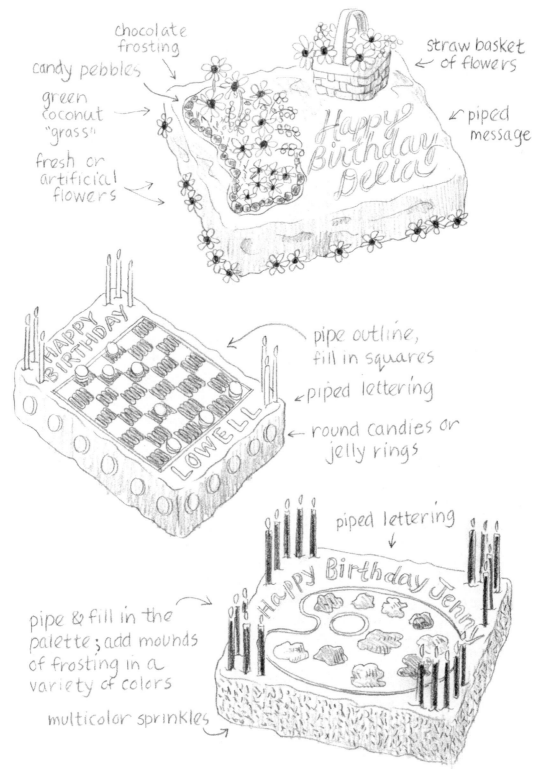

chocolate frosting

candy pebbles

green coconut "grass"

fresh or artificial flowers

straw basket of flowers

piped message

pipe outline, fill in squares

piped lettering

round candies or jelly rings

piped lettering

pipe & fill in the palette; add mounds of frosting in a variety of colors

multicolor sprinkles

117

ICE CREAM LAYER CAKE
WITH WHIPPED CREAM FROSTING

MAKES ONE FOUR-LAYER ROUND CAKE

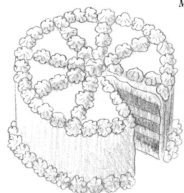

This cake consists of yellow or chocolate cake layers, ice cream filling and flavored whipped cream frosting. You can jazz up the filling by mixing some goodies (like chocolate chips or chopped nuts) into the softened ice cream before putting it between the cake layers.

Ice Cream Layer Cake is easy to prepare, since you can bake and freeze the cake layers well ahead of time. Put the cake layers and ice cream filling together a day ahead, too, if you like. In any case, you must allow several hours for the softened ice cream filling to freeze, so put the layers and filling together no later than the morning, for an afternoon party.

TIP: Before you begin, rearrange the items in your freezer to make space for the completed cake.

2 Layers of Yellow Layer Cake
(page 32) *or* 2 layers of Chocolate
Layer Cake (page 40)

For the filling:
3 pints of ice cream (see note
before step 1)
Extra ingredients for the filling
(optional; ½ cup per pint of ice
cream): chopped walnuts, pecans
or almonds; chocolate chips;
chopped semisweet or white
chocolate; crushed toffee candy;
toasted coconut

For the frosting and decoration:
3½–4 cups Vanilla, Chocolate
or Coffee Whipped Cream
(page 168)
Decorating bag and coupler
#30, #2D or other star tip

NOTE: For the filling, pick any ice cream flavors that are compatible with the cake. You need not pick three fancy flavors or even three different flavors; good old vanilla and chocolate are delicious in ice cream cake.

1. Wrap each cake layer snugly in plastic and freeze until firm. When firm, split each layer in half to make a total of four thin layers (how-to, page 20).

Put one thin layer cut side down on a large piece of aluminum foil and set the other three layers aside.

2. Take out one pint of ice cream and put it into a bowl. Let it soften enough to be mashed with a pastry blender; mash it just until pliable and then work it with a spatula until it is spreadable but not runny.

Stir in ½ cup of any extra ingredient chosen from the list above. Work quickly so the ice cream does not melt.

NOTE: If the ice cream does begin to melt, put the bowl in the freezer for a few minutes.

Spread the softened ice cream on the first cake layer. Place another cake layer cut side down on the ice cream, wrap the foil around the cake and freeze until the ice cream hardens.

Repeat step 2, using a pint of ice cream between each two cake layers. Wrap the four-layer cake completely in foil and freeze until hard.

3. Three hours before the party, make the flavored whipped cream. Place the cake on a serving platter and put strips of waxed paper under the cake to protect the platter (how-to, page 24). Use 2½–3 cups of whipped cream to frost the top and sides of the cake. Remove and discard the waxed paper strips. Put the rest of the whipped cream in the decorating bag fitted with the star tip and pipe rosettes on top of the cake and around the bottom as shown in the drawing at the beginning of the recipe.

Return the cake to the freezer (without covering or wrapping it) for at least two hours; take it out 20–30 minutes before serving time. Put candles on the cake and serve.

4 cake layers

3 cake layers

2 cake layers

wrap snugly & freeze

ICE CREAM CAKE ROLL
WITH RICH CHOCOLATE SAUCE

MAKES ONE ROLL ABOUT TEN INCHES LONG

Elegant and impressive—a delicate cake roll, filled with a pint of ice cream (and any extras you like—see below) and topped with mouth-watering chocolate sauce.

Ingredients for Old-Fashioned Jam Roll (page 100), except jam
1 pint of ice cream
Extra ingredients for the filling (optional; use about ¾ cup): chopped nuts (almonds, pistachios, pecans); chopped chocolate or chocolate chips; crushed toffee; rum-soaked raisins; toasted coconut; chopped fresh or frozen strawberries; whole fresh or frozen blueberries or raspberries

Rich Chocolate Sauce (recipe follows on page 121)

1. Follow the Old-Fashioned Jam Roll recipe, working through step 5. Let the rolled cake cool completely.

When the cake seems cool, unroll it and let it cool a little longer. (If it is warm, the ice cream filling will melt.)

2. Put the ice cream into a large bowl. Let it soften just enough to be mashed with a pastry blender; mash until it is pliable and then work it with a spatula until it is spreadable but not runny.

Working quickly, spread the softened ice cream on the cake roll. If desired, sprinkle on one or more of the extra ingredients listed above; press the ingredients into the ice cream with the spatula. Roll up the cake, using the towel to help.

Wrap the rolled cake snugly in aluminum foil and put it in the freezer to harden.

3. Meanwhile, make Rich Chocolate Sauce (recipe, page 121).

At serving time, take the cake out of the freezer and cut a thin slice off each end. Drizzle warm chocolate sauce over the cake and immediately sprinkle with nuts or a bit more of the extra ingredient used in the filling. Serve the remaining warm chocolate sauce in a separate bowl so guests can help themselves.

RICH CHOCOLATE SAUCE

MAKES ABOUT ONE CUP

One 5-ounce can of evaporated milk
2 ounces (2 squares) unsweetened chocolate, chopped
¾ cup sugar

2 tablespoons light corn syrup
Pinch of salt
2 tablespoons butter
½ teaspoon vanilla extract

1. Put the evaporated milk and chocolate in a medium-size saucepan over low heat. Cook, stirring and mashing, until the chocolate is melted and the mixture is as smooth as possible.

2. Add the sugar, corn syrup and salt and bring the mixture to a boil, stirring constantly. Simmer gently for five minutes, stirring often. The sauce will thicken somewhat as it cooks.

3. Strain the sauce into a small bowl and then return it to the saucepan. Let it cool slightly and stir in the butter and vanilla. The sauce will thicken considerably as it cools.

Refrigerate the sauce in the pan. At serving time, reheat the sauce to make it pourable; don't let it boil. Use the sauce while it is very warm, reheating it if necessary.

FANCY FROSTED CUPCAKES FOR KIDS

Sometimes it's a lot simpler—and more fun—to serve cupcakes to children, instead of cake. For instance, when your child has a birthday party at school, bring a tray of fancy cupcakes and you'll avoid the difficulties of cutting and serving a birthday cake. Making fancy cupcakes is a snap if you follow the 1-2-3 Plan below.

The decorations described and illustrated on the following pages are for adults (or older children) to make. For best results, read the Decorating Primer on pages 25–30 before you begin.

When kids are old enough to handle blunt plastic knives (age five and up), cupcake-decorating is a brief but lively party activity suitable for pint-sized attention spans. In the center of a table put a platter of unfrosted cupcakes and several small bowls of frosting. Set out little paper cups of decorative trimmings such as miniature chocolate chips, round candies, raisins, colored sprinkles, cinnamon redhots, etc. Let the children frost the cupcakes and press goodies into the frosting.

NOTE: If you plan to serve the decorated cupcakes later in the party, mark each child's initials on the bottom of the paper baking cup or otherwise identify each child's cupcake; this will save tears when it's time to eat.

1-2-3 PLAN

1. From the lists below, choose the cupcakes and frosting you want to make.

2. Look through the drawings and pick out one or more decorations. Assemble any special ingredients and utensils you will need.

3. Make the cupcakes and the frosting; tint the frosting, if desired. Frost the top of one cupcake and then decorate it immediately, before the frosting sets and forms a crust. Repeat for all the cupcakes.

CHOOSE CUPCAKES

The recipes suggested below give complete instructions for making cupcakes; if the recipe indicates a yield of only a few cupcakes plus a sheet cake, simply use all the batter for cupcakes instead.

NOTE: Use paper baking cups for lining the muffin pans.
- ◆ Yellow Layer Cake, page 32
- ◆ White Layer Cake, page 36
- ◆ Chocolate Layer Cake, page 40
- ◆ Burnt Sugar Layer Cake, page 44

CHOOSE A FROSTING

- ◆ Basic Vanilla Buttercream Frosting, page 162
- ◆ Easy Chocolate Buttercream Frosting, page 163
- ◆ Double Chocolate Frosting, page 167
- ◆ Vanilla Whipped Cream, page 168
- ◆ Chocolate Whipped Cream, page 168

CHOOSE DECORATIONS

chocolate
sprinkles
&
almond
slivers

straw

PAUL

paper
flag
&
sails

lifesaver

chocolate-
dipped
strawberry

animal
crackers

paper
parasol

simple
piping

licorice
drop

2 halves
of a round
cookie

almond
halves &
gumdrop

simple
piping

more

candle
&
colored
dots

candy bear
&
chocolate sprinkles

gumdrops

fresh
flower

cherry,
banana,
coconut

Instant Decorations

thin
mints

plastic toy

CHAPTER 9

Extravagant Cakes for Special Occasions

TWO-TIERED HEART CAKE FOR ROMANTIC OCCASIONS

BUTTER SPONGE TORTE WITH PECANS AND COFFEE CRUNCH FILLING

CELEBRATION CAKE

MINIATURE ICED CAKES

HAZELNUT CHEESECAKE

VANILLA MERINGUE CAKE WITH CREAM FILLING AND MERINGUE KISSES

CHOCOLATE GRAND MARNIER TORTE

In this chapter, "extravagant" refers more to time and effort than to money. Of course, a large cake for a party can be a costly undertaking, simply because it requires more ingredients. But some occasions clearly warrant the outlay of extra time, effort and money—and these cakes are worth every extra penny and minute they take.

A word about wedding cake: Should you be called upon to make a wedding cake, the recipe for the Two-Tiered Heart Cake (page 126) is perfect. If you like, add a third, smaller heart-shaped tier to the top and personalize the cake decorations for the wedding couple.

TWO-TIERED HEART CAKE
FOR ROMANTIC OCCASIONS

MAKES ONE LARGE CAKE, ABOUT 40 SERVINGS

A stunning and delicious cake for an engagement or wedding shower, anniversary celebration or Valentine's Day party.

BAKING PAN: ONE 8-INCH ROUND CAKE PAN; ONE 9-INCH ROUND CAKE PAN; ONE 8-INCH SQUARE CAKE PAN; ONE 9-INCH SQUARE CAKE PAN

PAN PREPARATION: GREASE AND FLOUR

PREHEAT OVEN TO 350°

BAKING TIME: 30–35 MINUTES

Ingredients for 2 recipes of White Layer Cake (page 36; see step 1)
¾–1 cup Apricot Glaze (page 173)
4½ cups Lemon or Orange Butter-cream Frosting (page 164)

For the decoration:
1 recipe Decorating Frosting (page 30)
Liquid or paste food coloring (optional)
1 or 2 decorating bags and couplers
#3 round tip; #30 closed star tip
Fresh flowers of your choice

NOTE: Before you begin this project, read all the recipes involved and read the Decorating Primer on pages 25–30 in Chapter 1. Also, have ready a large flat serving platter, at least 16 inches in diameter or 16 inches square, or a cake board (available in cake decorating stores or departments) of that size.

A good working plan is to bake the layers ahead of time, wrap them well and freeze them until the day of the party. Make the glaze and frostings on the day before the party and then you will be ready to go into production on the day itself.

1. Make two recipes of White Layer Cake batter; do *not* double the recipe—make it twice. Bake the first two pans of batter before you make the second batch.

The first time you make the batter, divide it between the prepared *8-inch round pan* and the prepared *9-inch square pan*. The pans should be equally full, so put a little more batter in the 9-inch pan; this will give you baked layers of approximately equal height. Bake as described in the cake recipe.

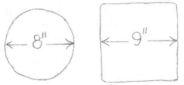

The second time you make the batter, divide it between the prepared *9-inch round pan* and the prepared *8-inch square pan*. Once again, put a little more batter in the 9-inch pan. Bake as described in the cake recipe.

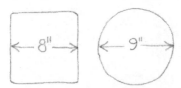

Wrap and freeze the layers as suggested in the note or wrap and freeze for an hour or two, until firm.

2. One at a time, remove the layers from the freezer and do the following:

● Cut a thin slice from the top of each layer to remove the browned part and to level off the layer.

● Square layers: Trim a thin slice from each side so no brown crust remains.

● Round layers: Cut each one in half and trim to remove the brown sides of each half-round.

● Brush away all the crumbs.

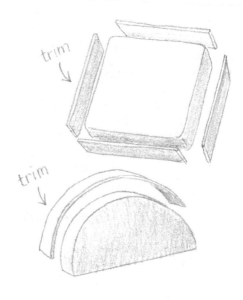

3. Place the larger square layer and the two larger half-rounds on the serving platter or cake board to make the larger heart, as shown in the diagram. If necessary, trim the top surfaces to make the cakes level with each other. Tuck waxed paper strips under the cake (how-to, page 24).

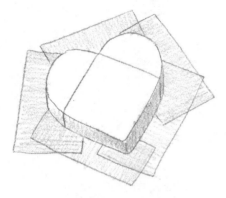

4. Warm the Apricot Glaze over low heat until it liquifies. Brush the entire heart-shaped layer—top and sides—with glaze. Do not soak the cake, but be sure it is completely coated, with a little extra glaze in the cracks between the pieces. Let the glaze dry for an hour.

5. When the glaze is dry or just slightly tacky, spread 2½–2¾ cups of Lemon or Orange Buttercream Frosting on the top and sides of the layer.

NOTE: The buttercream frosting is pale yellow (lemon) or pale peach-color (orange). If you would like to tint it, your best choices are a deeper yellow or a deeper peach (how to tint, page 24).

6. With the remaining cake, plan and make the second heart-shaped layer: On a table or counter, place the two smaller half-rounds against the smaller square layer. Level the tops and trim the half-rounds if necessary.

Place the smaller square layer on the frosted heart, leaving a one-inch ledge of frosted heart on each straight side. Put the smaller half-rounds in place against the square.

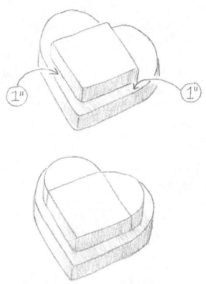

Carefully brush warm Apricot Glaze all over the top and sides of the smaller heart-shaped layer without dripping any on the frosted layer. Do not soak the cake, but be sure it is completely coated, with a little extra glaze in the cracks between the pieces. Let the glaze dry for at least an hour.

7. When the glaze is dry, or just slightly tacky, spread the remaining 1¾–2 cups of Lemon or Orange Buttercream Frosting on the top and sides of the smaller heart. It is difficult to keep the frosting neat where the top layer meets the bottom layer, but don't be concerned because that joint will be concealed by piped flowers.

8. Using Decorating Frosting, make the piped decorations on the cake: There are two parts to the piping—the dots and the flower borders. You can do all the piping in white (using the Decorating Frosting just as it is) or you can tint or color the Decorating Frosting to complement the fresh flowers you have chosen (how-to, page 24).

Here are some color suggestions for tinted piping on a cake frosted with yellow-tinted buttercream:

● Deep peach-color dots and deep peach-color flower borders

● Pale green dots and pink flower borders

● Lavender dots and deeper lavender flower borders

Here are some color suggestions for tinted or colored piping on a cake frosted with peach-color buttercream:

● Pale pink dots and deeper pink flower borders

● Red dots and red flower borders

● Pale blue dots and lavender flower borders

If you decide to use white or any other single color of piping, prepare and fill one decorating bag, attaching the #3 round tip.

If you decide to work with two colors, put ½ cup of Decorating Frosting in one bowl and the remaining Decorating Frosting in another bowl. Tint the smaller amount of frosting the color you have chosen for the dots and tint the larger amount the color you have chosen for the flower borders. Prepare and fill one decorating bag with the dot color, attaching the #3 tip. Prepare and fill a second decorating bag with the flower border color, attaching the #30 tip.

Pipe dots about ½ inch apart all over the cake, including the sides. Do this freehand and don't worry if the pattern is not perfectly regular. Remove and discard the waxed paper strips. Change to the #30 tip if you are working with one color.

With the #30 tip, pipe flowers all around the edges of both hearts, all around the cake where the two heart layers meet and around the base of the larger heart where it meets the serving platter or cake board. Refer to the drawing at the beginning of the recipe for guidance.

9. Prepare and add the fresh flowers just before presenting the cake: Cut off all but an inch of stem from the flower heads. Place flowers attractively around the ledge of the larger heart and arrange several in the center of the smaller heart. Tuck a few green leaves here and there for color contrast.

BUTTER SPONGE TORTE WITH PECANS AND COFFEE CRUNCH FILLING

MAKES A FOUR-LAYER ROUND CAKE

A scrumptious cake composed of four thin layers of butter sponge, brushed with rum and filled with coffee-flavored whipped cream and crunchy pieces of caramelized pecan.

BAKING PAN: TWO 9-INCH ROUND CAKE PANS

PAN PREPARATION: GREASE; LINE EACH PAN WITH A WAXED PAPER CIRCLE; GREASE THE WAXED PAPER CIRCLES; DUST THE PANS WITH FLOUR

PREHEAT OVEN TO 350°

BAKING TIME: 25–30 MINUTES

Ingredients for 1 recipe of Butter Sponge Layer Cake (page 34)
Caramelized Pecans (recipe follows on page 131)

1 tablespoon instant coffee granules
3 tablespoons superfine sugar
2 cups heavy cream, very cold
Light rum

1. Make the batter for Butter Sponge Layer Cake and bake it in the prepared 9-inch pans.

When the layers are cool, wrap them individually in plastic and freeze for an hour or two or until firm. Split each layer in half (how-to, page 20) to make a total of four thin layers.

2. Make the Caramelized Pecans and reserve 32 of the prettiest pecan halves for the top of the cake.

Break the rest of the pecans into pea-sized pieces: Put half the nuts at a time in a plastic bag; hold the bag shut and hit the pecans sharply with a mallet or the *blunt* edge of a heavy knife (e.g., a Chinese cleaver). Do not pulverize the nuts. Set them aside.

3. Make the Coffee Filling: Put the instant coffee granules in a small plastic bag and use a rolling pin to crush them to powder.

In a large bowl, whisk the coffee powder and the superfine sugar into the heavy cream. Keep whisking until the coffee dissolves completely. Beat the cream until stiff. Stir in the chopped caramelized pecans (not the reserved pecan halves).

4. Assemble the cake: Put the bottom half of one layer on a serving platter and brush with just enough rum to moisten the cake, not soak it. Spread a heaping cup of filling on the layer, working it out to the edges.

Repeat with the other three layers, ending with the top half of a layer and all the remaining filling. Decorate the top with the reserved pecan halves.

CARAMELIZED PECANS

BAKING PAN: ONE JELLY ROLL PAN AND ONE COOKIE SHEET
PAN PREPARATION: GREASE THE COOKIE SHEET LIGHTLY
WITH VEGETABLE OIL
PREHEAT OVEN TO 350°

2 cups pecan halves
¾ cup sugar
3 tablespoons water

1 teaspoon vanilla extract
1½ tablespoons butter

1. Spread the pecans on the ungreased jelly roll pan and toast them in the oven for ten minutes. Remove them and let them cool.

2. Put the sugar, water and vanilla in a heavy saucepan and bring slowly to a boil, stirring until the sugar has melted. Boil rapidly without stirring until the syrup reaches a temperature of 244°–248° (firm ball stage) on a candy thermometer. Remove the pan from the heat.

3. Add the pecans and stir to coat with syrup. Keep stirring—after less than a minute the mixture will begin to look whitish and sandy and the pecans will look frosted. Continue stirring for another half minute.

Put the saucepan over medium heat and continue to stir; the sugar will start to melt and caramelize. Keep stirring the pecans gently in the slowly-caramelizing sugar.

NOTE: Reduce the heat immediately if the mixture begins to smoke. Turn the heat up again when the smoking stops.

When the sugar has caramelized completely and the nuts are coated, turn off the heat and stir in the butter.

4. Turn the coated nuts onto the greased cookie sheet and spread them out in one layer. Let them cool completely and then break them apart.

CELEBRATION CAKE

MAKES A TWO-LAYER SHEET CAKE

A cake for a crowd, large enough to satisfy 20–25 cake-lovers—an extravaganza of lemon cake, Chocolate Pastry Cream filling and Chocolate Buttercream Frosting, decorated with mandarin orange segments.

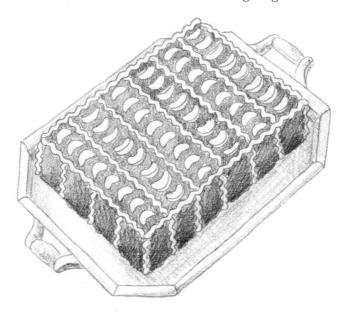

BAKING PAN: ONE 9 × 13 × 2-INCH SHEET CAKE PAN
PAN PREPARATION: GREASE AND FLOUR
PREHEAT OVEN TO 375°
BAKING TIME: 25 MINUTES

Ingredients for 2 recipes of Lemon
   Layer Cake (page 42)
½ cup Apricot Glaze (page 173)
1½ cups Chocolate Pastry Cream
   (page 171)
Two 15-ounce cans of mandarin
   orange segments

2½–3 cups Easy Chocolate Buttercream Frosting (page 163) *or*
   Chocolate Buttercream Frosting
   (page 163)
1 cup Decorating Frosting
   (page 30)
Decorating bag and coupler
#27 star tip

1. Make one recipe of Lemon Layer Cake and bake it in the prepared sheet cake pan, following the instructions on page 42. Let the cake cool in the pan for ten minutes on a wire rack and then turn it out carefully to finish cooling right side up on the rack.

When the cake is completely cool, slide it onto a large flat serving platter, tray or cake board. Tuck waxed paper strips under the layer (how-to, page 24). Set aside.

Wash and dry the sheet cake pan and prepare it again. Make the second recipe of Lemon Layer Cake; bake and cool it as described above. Set aside.

2. Brush warm Apricot Glaze on the top and sides of the first cake layer and let the glaze dry for one hour.

3. Spread all the Chocolate Pastry Cream evenly on the top of the first layer, not quite to the edges.

Drain the liquid from both cans of mandarin orange segments and spread the segments on paper towels to dry. Pick out 48 perfect segments and set them aside for decorating the top of the cake. Arrange a layer of mandarin orange segments on the pastry cream, using as many of the remaining segments as will fit without overlapping.

Cover with the second cake layer.

4. Brush warm Apricot Glaze on the top and sides of the second layer and let the glaze dry for one hour.

5. Spread all of the chocolate buttercream evenly over the top and sides of the cake.

6. Fit the decorating bag with the coupler and #27 star tip (see Decorating Primer, page 27) and fill the bag with Decorating Frosting.

Use a toothpick to draw five faint lines on top of the cake, dividing it in sixths. Pipe wavy lines over the toothpick lines.

Continue the wavy lines down the long sides of the cake, referring to the drawing on page 132 for guidance. Pipe wavy lines on the short sides of the cake, too. Edge the long sides of the top of the cake with wavy lines.

Place eight mandarin orange segments in each section of the top of the cake, all eight segments facing the same direction, as shown in the drawing.

Refrigerate the cake until half an hour before serving.

MINIATURE ICED CAKES

MAKES ABOUT 40 SMALL CAKES

Serve this simplified but elegant version of petits fours at an afternoon tea, wedding lunch or other memorable occasion. The iced cakes may be made ahead and frozen.

BAKING PAN: ONE 8-INCH SQUARE PAN AND ONE 9-INCH SQUARE PAN

PAN PREPARATION: GREASE; LINE THE BOTTOMS WITH WAXED PAPER; GREASE THE WAXED PAPER; DUST THE PANS WITH FLOUR

PREHEAT OVEN TO 350°

BAKING TIME: 25 MINUTES FOR 8-INCH LAYER; 30 MINUTES FOR 9-INCH LAYER

Ingredients for 1 recipe of Butter Sponge Layer Cake (page 34)
Apricot jam and seedless raspberry jam
Covering Icing (recipe follows on page 135)
Red and yellow liquid food coloring

For the decoration (choose any of these):
Pecan halves, whole almonds, hazelnuts or pistachios
Small pieces of glacé fruit (apricot, cherry, orange)
Small, pretty candies (miniature nonpareils, Jordan almonds, candied violets, etc.)
Whole, perfect berries or halved grapes

1. Make the batter for Butter Sponge Layer Cake and pour it into the two prepared pans; the batter should be the same depth in both pans, so put a bit more in the larger pan.

Bake the two layers at the same time, leaving the 8-inch pan in the oven for 25 minutes and the 9-inch pan for 30 minutes or until a cake tester inserted in the center of the cake comes out clean. Let the layers cool in the pans on wire racks for ten minutes and then turn out to finish cooling right side up on the racks.

Cut a thin slice off each side of each layer to eliminate the crisp edges.

2. Use a 1½-inch round biscuit cutter to cut the 8-inch layer into 16 rounds, leaving ¼ inch between rounds. To get a clean cut, swivel the cutter as you press down.

Cut the 9-inch layer in squares and diamonds: Use a ruler and sharp knife to cut 1½-inch squares. The diamonds should be about 1½ inches wide and two inches long.

3. Warm the apricot jam in a small saucepan and strain it; in another small saucepan, warm and stir the raspberry jam until it is smooth.

Split each little cake in half, spread the bottom half with apricot or raspberry jam and put the halves back together.

4. Prepare Covering Icing. Keep it quite warm (not hot, not lukewarm) over the hot water in the bottom of the double boiler. Add two drops each of yellow and red food coloring and stir well to make pale peach-color icing.

NOTE: If the icing thickens during the process of coating the cakes, warm it by reheating the hot water in the bottom of the double boiler and then thin the icing with a few drops of water and a few drops of light corn syrup. It must be warm and as thin as heavy cream or it will not coat the cakes properly.

5. Ice and decorate the cakes: First, place a large piece of waxed paper on the counter or table, put your chosen decorations in small bowls close at hand and have ready a ½-inch pastry brush. Place a wire rack over a large bowl and set three of the cakes on it. Put the double boiler (with the warm icing in the top) near the wire rack.

Hold one cake and brush icing all around the sides, covering them completely. Set the cake on the rack and pour a spoonful of icing on top, letting the excess drip down the sides of the cake and into the bowl.

Try to work quickly. (This process may seem a little tricky at first, but it will get easier with practice.)

Press one of the decorations firmly into the icing; the icing will harden with the decoration firmly embedded.

Repeat the icing and decorating procedure with the other two cakes. Use a short, wide spatula to transfer each finished cake to the piece of waxed paper.

Ice and decorate the rest of the cakes in the same manner. When the icing in the double boiler is used up, scoop the icing that has dripped into the bowl back into the top of the double boiler and reheat it (thinning it if necessary). Use the reheated icing to finish the remaining cakes.

Serve the cakes on a doily-lined tray.

COVERING ICING

MAKES ABOUT 3½ CUPS

7 tablespoons water
7 tablespoons light corn syrup
2 teaspoons vanilla
6 cups sifted confectioners' sugar

1. Stir the water, corn syrup and vanilla together in the top pan of a double boiler. Gradually add the confectioners' sugar, beating until smooth.

2. Fill the bottom pan of the double boiler half full of water and bring it to a simmer. Fit the top pan over the bottom and stir the icing until it is very warm and perfectly smooth. It should be as thin as heavy cream.

Turn off the heat but leave the icing over the water. Reheat the water occasionally to keep the icing thin.

HAZELNUT CHEESECAKE

MAKES ONE 9-INCH CAKE

A rich, elegant, heavenly cheesecake, guaranteed to impress your guests.

TIP: Make this cake at a time when you can use the oven for four hours without interruption; once you start baking, you should not take the cheesecake out of the oven for even a moment (see step 6).

BAKING PAN: ONE 9-INCH SPRINGFORM PAN

PAN PREPARATION: SEE STEP 1

PREHEAT OVEN TO 300°

BAKING TIME: 75 MINUTES; TOTAL OF
THREE HOURS AND 45 MINUTES IN THE OVEN

For the crust:
¾ cup ground hazelnuts (see note before step 1)
½ cup honey graham cracker crumbs (about three whole crackers)
Pinch of salt
¼ cup butter, melted and cooled

For the filling:
1½ pounds (three 8-ounce packages) cream cheese, softened
1 cup sugar
¼ cup flour
¼ teaspoon salt
1 teaspoon vanilla extract
¼ teaspoon almond extract
4 eggs, separated
½ cup heavy cream
½ teaspoon grated lemon rind
1 cup ground hazelnuts (see note before step 1)

NOTE: Before grinding the hazelnuts, toast and rub them to remove as much papery skin as possible (how-to, page 17).

1. Prepare the springform pan: Cut four pieces of aluminum foil, each 16 inches long. Stack them, centered, in different directions as shown in the drawing. Put the springform pan in the center of the stack and press the foil up tightly around the pan, folding the corners of the foil down even with the rim of the pan. Be careful not to puncture the foil, since this aluminum foil jacket will protect the contents of the pan when you place the pan in a water bath for baking.

Grease the pan.

2. Make the crust: Stir the crust ingredients together in a small bowl. Put the mixture in the prepared pan and pat it evenly over the bottom of the pan. Set the pan in the refrigerator.

3. In a large bowl, beat the softened cream cheese until smooth and light. Add ¾ cup of the sugar, the flour, salt, vanilla and almond extracts and beat until well blended.

4. Add the egg yolks and beat until smooth. Add the heavy cream and grated lemon rind and beat just until blended. Stir in the ground hazelnuts.

5. Fill a kettle with water and bring it to a boil.

Meanwhile, finish making the filling: In another large bowl, with clean, dry beaters, beat the egg whites until foamy. Add the remaining ¼ cup of sugar and beat until the egg whites hold firm, glossy, moist peaks. Fold a third of the beaten whites into the cream cheese mixture to lighten it; fold the rest of the whites into the lightened cream cheese mixture. Carefully pour the filling onto the crust in the pan.

Place the filled springform pan in a larger pan (for instance, a broiler pan) on the center rack of the oven. Fill the larger pan with boiling water to a depth of one inch. Be careful not to get any water in the springform pan.

6. Bake the cheesecake for 75 minutes. Do not insert a cake tester and *do not remove the cake from the oven.*

Turn off the heat and leave the cake in the still-hot oven with the oven door closed for 30 minutes. Then prop the oven door open just a little, using the handle of a wooden spoon, and leave the cheesecake in the slowly cooling oven for two more hours. Be patient with this process; it produces a cake that is perfectly baked, with a minimum of cracking on top.

Remove both pans from the oven and lift the springform pan out of the water bath. Remove the aluminum foil jacket and let the cake cool completely in the springform pan on a wire rack. When it is cool, run a knife carefully around the sides of the cake and then release and remove the sides of the pan.

Leave the cheesecake on the bottom of the springform pan and refrigerate it. When the cake is cold, run a long metal spatula under the crust to loosen it from the pan; slide the cake onto a round platter. Let it come to room temperature before serving.

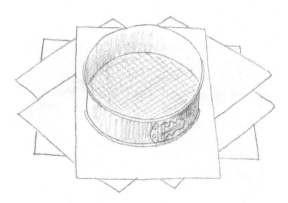

VANILLA MERINGUE CAKE
WITH CREAM FILLING AND MERINGUE KISSES

MAKES A THREE-LAYER ROUND CAKE

A luscious, melt-in-your-mouth confection composed of three meringue layers and your favorite flavor of cream filling.

TIP: Don't try to make this cake on a hot or humid day—meringue requires cool, dry weather.

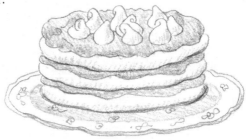

BAKING PAN: ONE COOKIE SHEET AND TWO 8-INCH ROUND CAKE PANS

PAN PREPARATION: GREASE AND FLOUR THE COOKIE SHEET; DRAW AN 8-INCH CIRCLE ON THE COOKIE SHEET BY OUTLINING A CAKE PAN WITH A TOOTHPICK; GREASE AND FLOUR THE UNDERSIDES OF THE CAKE PANS

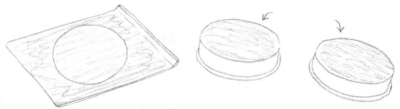

PREHEAT OVEN TO 250°
BAKING TIME: 40 MINUTES; TOTAL OF ONE HOUR AND 40 MINUTES IN THE OVEN

For the meringue layers:
1 cup superfine sugar
½ cup confectioners' sugar
5 eggs whites
Pinch of salt
¼ teaspoon cream of tartar
½ teaspoon fresh lemon juice
1 teaspoon vanilla extract
Large decorating bag and coupler
½-inch round tip

For the filling, topping and decoration:
¾ cup heavy cream, very cold
2 teaspoons sugar
1¼ cups pastry cream, any favorite flavor (pages 170–171)
Grated chocolate, slivered almonds or shredded coconut (optional)

1. Sift together the superfine sugar and confectioners' sugar. Put half the mixture in a second bowl and set both bowls aside.

2. Make the meringue: Combine the egg whites, salt, cream of tartar, lemon juice and vanilla and beat until the whites hold soft peaks. Add one bowl of the sugar mixture (¾ cup), one tablespoon at a time, beating until the whites are thick and smooth and stand in firm, glossy, moist peaks.

Gradually fold in the remaining sugar mixture.

3. Fit the decorating bag with the ½-inch round tip and fill the bag with half the meringue (how-to, page 27). Pipe a circle of meringue just inside the edge of each inverted cake pan and just inside the inscribed circle on the cookie sheet. Pipe 12 small meringue kisses on the cookie sheet. Squeeze back into the bowl any meringue left in the decorating bag.

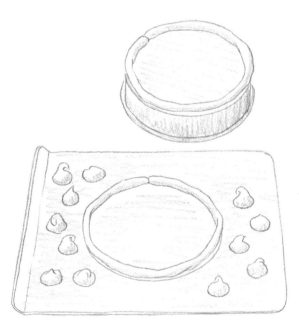

Now spoon a third of the remaining meringue in the center of each piped circle and spread it out evenly to meet the piped circle and form a ½-inch-thick layer.

4. Bake all three layers at the same time, for 40 minutes. Turn off the heat and leave the meringues in the closed oven for another hour to dry completely.

Remove the pans from the oven and run a long spatula under each layer to loosen it. Carefully slide the layers onto wire racks to finish cooling. The cooled kisses can be twisted and lifted right off the cookie sheet.

5. Make the cream filling: Put the heavy cream and sugar in a bowl and beat until stiff. Fold a third of the whipped cream into the pastry cream to lighten it; fold the remaining whipped cream into the lightened pastry cream. Refrigerate the filling until you are ready to assemble the cake.

6. Assemble the cake about one hour before serving: Place one meringue layer on a serving platter and spread a third of the cream filling on it. Cover with the second layer and another third of the filling. Top with the third layer and all the remaining filling. Arrange eight or ten of the prettiest meringue kisses on top of the cake, pressing them gently into the cream filling.

If you like, sprinkle the top with grated chocolate, slivered almonds or shredded coconut.

NOTE: The longer the assembled cake stands before being eaten, the softer the meringue layers become. Ideally, it will be served not more than two hours after being assembled, so that the cake will be a wonderful combination of crunchy and chewy textures.

CHOCOLATE GRAND MARNIER TORTE

MAKES A TWO-LAYER ROUND CAKE

Definitely a sophisticated cake—two dense, dark chocolate layers moistened with liqueur, topped with orange marmalade and covered with bittersweet chocolate glaze.

BAKING PAN: TWO 9-INCH ROUND CAKE PANS

PAN PREPARATION: GREASE AND FLOUR

PREHEAT OVEN TO 350°

BAKING TIME: 25–30 MINUTES

4 ounces (4 squares) semisweet
 chocolate
3 ounces (3 squares) unsweetened
 chocolate
½ cup butter
2 teaspoons vanilla extract
6 eggs, separated
1 whole egg
1 cup sugar
1 tablespoon grated orange rind
¼ teaspoon salt
1 teaspoon cream of tartar
¼ cup cake flour

For the filling and topping:
5 tablespoons Grand Marnier
 liqueur
½ cup orange marmalade
Easy Bittersweet Chocolate Glaze
 (page 172)

For the decoration:
8 or more glacé orange slices

1. In a heavy saucepan, melt the chocolate and butter over low heat, stirring until smooth. Turn off the heat, add the vanilla and stir again. Set aside to cool.

2. In a large bowl, combine the six egg yolks and the whole egg. Add all but two tablespoons of the sugar (a total of 14 tablespoons), one tablespoon at a time, beating well after each addition. When all the sugar is incorporated, beat for two more minutes at medium speed.

3. Add the cooled chocolate mixture, grated orange rind and salt and beat at low speed to combine.

4. In another large bowl, with clean, dry beaters, beat the six egg whites until foamy. Add the remaining two tablespoons of sugar and the cream of tartar and beat until the whites hold firm, glossy, moist peaks. Fold about a third of the egg whites into the chocolate batter to lighten it; fold the rest of the egg whites into the lightened batter.

5. Using a fine strainer, sift the cake flour into the batter a little at a time, folding it in gently. Divide the batter equally between the two prepared pans.

6. Bake for 25–30 minutes or until a cake tester inserted in the center of the cake comes out clean. (The layers may be puffed and uneven, but don't worry about this because they will flatten and even out as they cool.) Let the layers cool in the pans on wire racks for ten minutes and then turn them out to finish cooling right side up on the racks.

7. When the layers are completely cool, level each one by slicing off the high spots. If necessary, slice off a little more to remove any crusty bits left on the top of each layer.

Leave one layer right side up on the wire rack; invert the second layer so the wrong side—which should be quite smooth—becomes the top. (This smooth side will be the top of the torte, a foundation for the shiny glaze.) Level the smooth side of the layer, then peel and brush away any crumbs and loose pieces of cake.

With the cake still on the wire racks, brush two tablespoons of liqueur on the top of each layer, letting the liqueur soak in before brushing more on. Be sure to brush all the way to the edges.

8. Mix the orange marmalade with the remaining tablespoon of liqueur. Spread half the marmalade mixture on the first layer and top it with the second layer; spread the rest of the marmalade mixture on the second layer.

9. Cover the entire cake with Easy Bittersweet Chocolate Glaze: Set the wire rack over a cookie sheet. Pour ½ cup of glaze onto the center of the cake and use a metal spatula to spread it evenly over the top. Pour more glaze around the very edge of the cake so the glaze drips down the sides and onto the cookie sheet. Use the spatula to scoop up excess glaze from the cookie sheet and spread it on the bare spots on the sides.

Decorate the top of the torte with glacé orange slices, arranging them in your own design or following one of the drawings below.

The glaze will take several hours to set and it will remain glossy as long as you do not refrigerate the torte. If you refrigerate it, the glaze will harden and take on a matte finish.

OTHER EXTRAVAGANT CAKES TO MAKE:

Mocha Sponge Roll with Chestnut Filling and Chocolate Glaze, page 58
Raspberries-and-Cream Cake, page 88
Fresh Coconut Layer Cake, page 108
Glazed Nut Cake with Almond Paste Fruits, page 147

CHAPTER 10

Christmas Cakes

HOLIDAY JAM CAKE WITH SUGARPLUMS

CHRISTMAS TREE CAKE

GLAZED NUT CAKE WITH ALMOND PASTE FRUITS

WHISKEY FRUITCAKE

FIGGY FRUITCAKE WITH HARD SAUCE

CHRISTMAS RUM RING

GINGERBREAD COTTAGE

YULE LOG

Next to champagne and Santa Claus, nothing is more welcome at a Christmas dinner or party than a festive, homemade cake. Many of the recipes in this book would be appropriate for Christmas, but the cakes in this chapter have a special look and taste that make them perfect for holiday entertaining.

One friendly, hospitable way to spread holiday cheer is to give a dessert party: Serve eggnog or sparkling punch and an array of handsome Christmas cakes—perhaps a Figgy Fruitcake, a Glazed Nut Cake and a Christmas Tree Cake. Let guests help themselves while you sit back and enjoy the compliments.

HOLIDAY JAM CAKE WITH SUGARPLUMS

MAKES A TWO-LAYER ROUND CAKE

A traditional spice cake with a cup of jam mixed right into the batter. Give it an old-fashioned look with fluffy white Snowdrift Frosting and a decoration of homemade "sugarplums." If you like, make layers ahead, wrap them well and stash them in the freezer for unexpected guests.

BAKING PAN: TWO 8-INCH ROUND CAKE PANS
PAN PREPARATION: GREASE AND FLOUR
PREHEAT OVEN TO 350°
BAKING TIME: 35 MINUTES

2 cups flour
1½ teaspoons baking powder
½ teaspoon baking soda
½ teaspoon salt
½ teaspoon cinnamon
¼ teaspoon nutmeg
¼ teaspoon ground cloves
½ cup (1 stick) butter, softened
½ cup light brown sugar
2 eggs

¼ cup buttermilk
1 cup seedless blackberry jam (see note before step 1)
2¼ cups Snowdrift Frosting (page 166)

For the sugarplums:
12 whole pitted prunes
Sugar

NOTE: If you can't find seedless blackberry jam, warm and strain one 18-ounce jar or two 12-ounce jars of blackberry jam with seeds; measure out one cup of strained jam.

1. Stir or whisk together the flour, baking powder, baking soda, salt and spices; set aside.

2. In a large bowl, cream the butter until light. Add the brown sugar gradually, beating well after each addition.

3. Add the eggs one at a time, beating well after each addition.

4. Add about half of the dry ingredients and blend just until moistened. Add the buttermilk and mix well. Add the rest of the dry ingredients and blend again.

5. Stir in the jam thoroughly. Divide the batter equally between the two prepared pans.

6. Bake for 35 minutes or until a cake tester inserted in the center of the cake comes out clean. Let the layers cool in the pans on wire racks for ten minutes and then turn out to finish cooling right side up on the wire racks.

7. Fill the cake with a scant cup of the Snowdrift Frosting; frost the top and sides with the rest of the frosting. Do not refrigerate the cake.

Just before serving the cake, cut each prune in half and dredge each half in sugar to make the sugarplums. Arrange the sugarplums neatly on top of the cake.

CHRISTMAS TREE CAKE

MAKES A TWO-LAYER CAKE

A festive addition to any Christmas party. Decorate as described here or invent your own special trimmings, consulting the Decorating Primer on pages 25–30.

BAKING PAN: ONE 10½ × 15½ × 1-INCH JELLY ROLL PAN

PAN PREPARATION: GREASE AND FLOUR

PREHEAT OVEN TO 375°

BAKING TIME: 20–25 MINUTES

Ingredients for 1 recipe of Yellow Layer Cake (page 32)
2½ cups Basic Vanilla Buttercream Frosting (page 162)
Green paste food coloring
Chopped walnuts, pecans or almonds
Small round red or multi-colored candies (cinnamon redhots, imperials, etc.)
Decorating bag and coupler
#7 or other favorite tip

1. Make the batter for Yellow Layer Cake and pour all but ½ cup into the prepared jelly roll pan; the batter should fill the pan about half full. (Discard the unused ½ cup of batter.) Bake for 20–25 minutes or until a cake tester inserted in the center comes out clean.

Let the cake cool for ten minutes in the pan on a large wire rack and then carefully turn it out to finish cooling right side up on the rack.

2. When the cake is cool, slide it onto a flat surface and trim a thin slice from each side. Have ready a large flat serving platter or 13 × 19-inch cake board.

Cut the cake in five pieces as shown in the diagram. Assemble pieces 1, 2 and 3 right side up on the platter or cake board, centering them as shown. Tuck waxed paper strips under the cake (how-to, page 24).

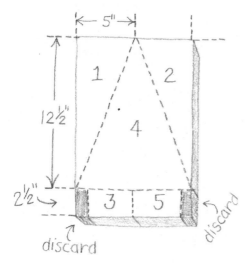

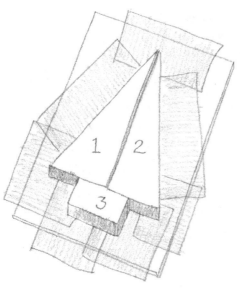

3. Spread ¾ cup of Basic Vanilla Buttercream Frosting on the *top* (not the sides) of the tree and trunk. Put pieces 4 and 5 wrong side up on the frosted cake layer.

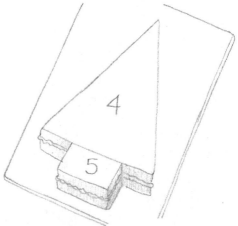

4. Tint the remaining frosting light green. Use 1¼ cups of the light green frosting to cover the top and sides of the tree. Press chopped nuts into the frosting on all sides of the cake and on top of the trunk.

5. Tint the remaining ½ cup of light green frosting a darker green. Attach the tip to the decorating bag and fill the bag with the darker green frosting (how-to, page 27). Pipe dark green loops on the tree and then press the small candies into the light green frosting as shown in the drawing at the beginning of the recipe.

Pull out the waxed paper strips very slowly so you don't dislodge the trunk of the tree.

Surround the cake with greens or garlands and tuck a few shiny Christmas balls into the garlands.

GLAZED NUT CAKE
WITH ALMOND PASTE FRUITS

MAKES A 9-INCH ROUND CAKE

Densely packed with toasted almonds and hazelnuts, coated with a glossy honey glaze and decorated with a colorful wreath of almond paste fruits—this small, special Christmas cake tastes as good as it looks.

TIP: You may substitute store-bought marzipan fruits for the homemade almond paste fruits used in this recipe.

BAKING PAN: ONE 9-INCH ROUND CAKE PAN
PAN PREPARATION: GREASE AND FLOUR
PREHEAT OVEN TO 350°
BAKING TIME: 45–50 MINUTES

1½ cups almonds, toasted (how-to, page 17)
1½ cups hazelnuts, toasted and rubbed (how-to, page 17)
1½ cups flour
1 teaspoon baking powder
½ teaspoon baking soda
½ teaspoon salt
2 tablespoons fresh lemon juice
2 teaspoons grated lemon rind
⅓ cup brandy
½ cup (1 stick) butter, softened
½ cup light brown sugar
6 tablespoons honey

1 egg beaten with one additional egg white
1 teaspoon vanilla extract

Honey Glaze (recipe follows on page 148)
Almond Paste Fruits (recipe follows on page 149)

1. Coarsely chop the toasted almonds and hazelnuts; set aside. Stir or whisk together the flour, baking powder, baking soda and salt; set aside. In another bowl, stir together the lemon juice, grated lemon rind and brandy; set aside.

2. In a large bowl, cream the butter until light. Gradually add the brown sugar, beating well after each addition. Add the honey and beat again.

3. Pour in the beaten eggs and vanilla and beat well.

4. Add about half of the flour mixture and stir well; add the brandy mixture and stir again. Add the rest of the flour mixture and stir until thoroughly blended.

5. Stir in the chopped nuts. Spoon the batter into the prepared pan and spread it evenly.

6. Bake for 45–50 minutes or until a cake tester inserted in the center of the cake comes out clean. Let the cake cool in the pan on a wire rack for ten minutes and then turn it out to finish cooling right side up on the rack.

7. When the cake is just warm, put it on a serving platter. Tuck waxed paper strips under the cake to protect the platter (how-to, page 24). Pour all the Honey Glaze onto the center of the cake and spread it so that it covers the top and drips down the sides. Use a small metal spatula to scoop up excess glaze from the platter and spread it on the sides of the cake.

Let the cake stand for a few minutes to allow excess glaze to collect again on the waxed paper. Discard the excess glaze or save it for another use. Remove and discard the waxed paper strips.

8. While the glaze is still sticky, decorate the top of the cake with Almond Paste Fruits (page 149): On a piece of waxed paper, arrange fruits, berries and leaves, following the design shown below. Lift each fruit (not the leaves or berries) and slice off a small piece to make a flat surface. Transfer the fruits, berries and leaves to the cake, pressing each one in place.

The cake is extremely crumbly while it is warm, so be sure the cake is completely cool before you serve it.

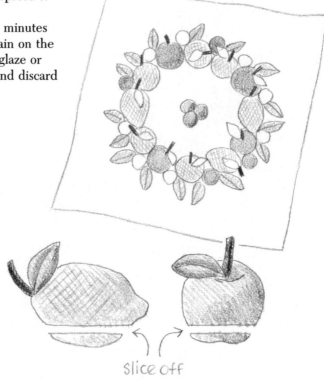

slice off small pieces

HONEY GLAZE

MAKES ABOUT ½ CUP

1 tablespoon butter
¼ cup honey
2 tablespoons brandy
⅔ cup confectioners' sugar

In a small saucepan, warm the butter, honey and brandy over low heat and stir until blended. Remove from the heat, transfer to a bowl and let the mixture cool. Beat in the confectioners' sugar.

ALMOND PASTE FRUITS

One 8-ounce can of pure almond paste

Paste food colors (red, yellow, orange and bright green)
12–15 whole cloves

1. Divide the almond paste into four balls. Use a toothpick to smear a little red food coloring on one ball and work it in thoroughly with your fingers; if necessary, add more coloring to make a brighter red. Repeat this procedure with the other balls of almond paste and the other colors, to make balls of yellow, orange and green.

NOTE: Because the almond paste is not pure white, the colors you make will not be bright and clear; just mix in enough paste food coloring to make a fairly intense color.

Wrap each ball in plastic wrap and leave it wrapped when you are not using it. Rinse your fingers often while working with the sticky almond paste.

2. Make four or five apples: With red almond paste, roll balls one inch in diameter; with green almond paste, shape small leaves. Indent the top of each ball, press a leaf near the indentation and push a clove into the top for the stem.

3. Repeat step 2, using orange almond paste to make four or five oranges. However, before adding the leaves, press all sides of each ball into the wire mesh of a strainer to simulate the rough texture of a real orange.

4. Repeat step 2, using yellow almond paste to make three or four lemons. Mold each ball into a more elongated shape as shown in the drawing and, before adding the leaves, press all sides into the wire mesh of a strainer to simulate the rough texture of a real lemon.

5. With the remaining almond paste make more green leaves and several small berries of each color.

WHISKEY FRUITCAKE

MAKES TWO LOAVES

This is a soft, tender fruitcake, a heady concoction of bourbon-soaked bits of dried fruit baked in a brown sugar and molasses cake batter. This is *not* a long-lasting fruitcake, so eat it soon after baking.

BAKING PAN: TWO 9½ × 5½ × 2¾-INCH LOAF PANS
OR A SELECTION OF REGULAR AND MINIATURE LOAF PANS
IN SIZES SUITABLE FOR MAKING GIFT LOAVES

PAN PREPARATION: GREASE AND FLOUR

PREHEAT OVEN TO 300°

BAKING TIME: 75–80 MINUTES

1 cup dark raisins
1 cup golden raisins
1 cup chopped pitted dates
1 cup dried currants
1 cup chopped dried apricots
1½ cups bourbon whiskey
2½ cups flour
½ teaspoon baking powder
¼ teaspoon baking soda
½ teaspoon salt
1 teaspoon cinnamon
½ teaspoon nutmeg
¼ teaspoon ground cloves

2 tablespoons fresh lemon juice
2 teaspoons grated lemon rind
2 teaspoons grated orange rind
1 cup (2 sticks) butter, softened
1½ cups dark brown sugar
2 tablespoons unsulphured molasses
6 eggs, beaten

For the decoration (optional):
Light corn syrup
Glacé fruits
Pecan or walnut halves, whole
   almonds

NOTE: At least one day before baking the fruitcakes, put the dried fruits (chopped as indicated) in a big bowl and pour one cup of the bourbon over them. Mix well, cover with plastic wrap and set aside for 24–48 hours, stirring occasionally, to absorb the bourbon.

1. Stir or whisk together the flour, baking powder, baking soda, salt and spices; set aside. Stir the lemon juice, grated lemon rind and grated orange rind into the remaining ½ cup of bourbon; set aside.

2. In a large bowl, cream the butter until light. Gradually add the brown sugar, beating well after each addition. Add the molasses and blend well.

3. Pour in the beaten eggs a little at a time, beating well after each addition. When all the eggs have been incorporated, beat for two more minutes at high speed.

4. Add the bourbon–lemon juice mixture and the dry ingredients alternately, in three parts each, beating well after each addition.

5. Stir the bourbon-soaked fruits into the batter. Divide the batter equally between the two prepared loaf pans *or*, if you are making a variety of smaller loaves, fill each prepared pan a little more than half full of batter.

6. Bake 9½ × 5½ × 2¾-inch loaves for 75–80 minutes; if you are using a variety of pans, adjust the baking times accordingly. Loaves are done when a cake tester inserted in the center of each loaf comes out free of batter, even though it may have some sticky fruit particles clinging to it.

Let the cakes cool in the pans on wire racks for ten minutes and then turn out to finish cooling right side up on the racks.

7. Decorate the top of each fruitcake: Following the diagrams below, arrange nuts and pieces of glacé fruit on the cake. Pick up each nut and piece of fruit, brush the back with light corn syrup and replace it on the cake. Serve within a week, with or without Hard Sauce (page 152).

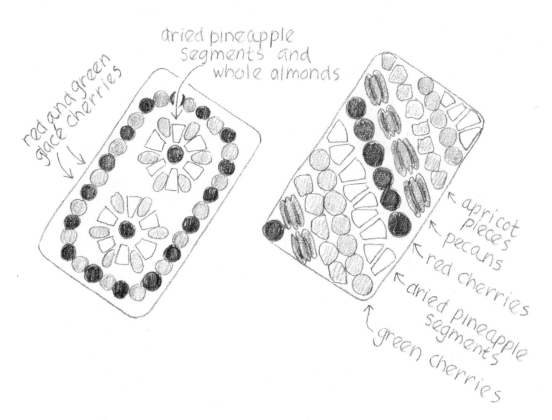

FIGGY FRUITCAKE WITH HARD SAUCE

MAKES ONE 9-INCH RING

A light fruitcake, flavored with brandy and generously studded with chunks of fig. Slice and serve warm, with dollops of Hard Sauce.

BAKING PAN: ONE 9-INCH FLUTED TUBE CAKE PAN, 3¾ INCHES DEEP
PAN PREPARATION: GREASE AND FLOUR
PREHEAT OVEN TO 300°
BAKING TIME: 70 MINUTES

2½ cups chopped dried figs
2¼ cups flour
1 teaspoon baking powder
½ teaspoon salt
½ cup (1 stick) butter, softened
1 cup sugar

3 eggs beaten with one additional
  egg yolk
1 teaspoon grated lemon rind
½ cup brandy

Hard Sauce (recipe below)

1. Spread the chopped figs on a piece of waxed paper. Sprinkle ¼ cup of the flour over them. With your fingers, toss and separate the bits of fig to coat them lightly with flour. Put the figs in a bowl, discarding any excess flour.

Stir or whisk together the remaining two cups of flour, the baking powder and salt; set aside.

2. In a large bowl, cream the butter until light. Gradually add the sugar, beating well after each addition.

3. Pour in the beaten eggs a little at a time, beating well after each addition. Add the grated lemon rind and blend well.

4. Add the dry ingredients and the brandy alternately, in three parts each, blending well after each addition. Stir the chopped figs into the batter. Pour and spoon the batter into the prepared pan.

5. Bake for 70 minutes or until a cake tester inserted in the center of the cake comes out free of batter; the tester may have some sticky fig clinging to it.

Let the cake cool in the pan on a wire rack for ten minutes and then turn it out to finish cooling rounded side up on the rack.

Serve warm with a spoonful of cold or room-temperature Hard Sauce on each slice.

HARD SAUCE

MAKES ABOUT ONE CUP

½ cup (1 stick) butter, softened
1 cup confectioners' sugar
1 tablespoon of brandy

Cream the butter until light. Gradually beat in the confectioners' sugar to make a firm paste. Beat in the brandy. Cover and store the Hard Sauce in the refrigerator; let it soften slightly or bring it to room temperature before serving.

CHRISTMAS RUM RING

MAKES ONE 10½-INCH TUBE CAKE

You may recognize the Christmas Rum Ring as a French cake called a *savarin*, a light yeast cake that requires only one period of rising and no kneading at all.

BAKING PAN: 10½-INCH TUBE PAN, THREE INCHES DEEP
PAN PREPARATION: GREASE
PREHEAT OVEN TO 400° AFTER BATTER HAS RISEN
BAKING TIME: 20–25 MINUTES

¼ cup warm water (see step 1)
1 package (¼ ounce; scant table-
    spoon) dry yeast
3 eggs
2 tablespoons sugar
½ teaspoon salt
¼ cup hot milk
2 cups flour
10 tablespoons butter, softened

For the rum syrup:
1 cup sugar
1½ cups water
1 cup rum

For the frosting and decoration:
½ cup Apricot Glaze (page 173)
**Rum Frosting (recipe follows on
    page 154)**
Red and green glacé cherries
Decorating bag and coupler
#30 or other star tip

1. Prepare the yeast by dissolving it in water at a temperature between 105° and 115°: First fill a measuring cup with warm water and test it with an instant-reading thermometer; it should feel warm on your fingertips, not hot or cool. Adjust the temperature if necessary by pouring off some water and then adding either hot or cold water until the thermometer reads between 105° and 115°. When you have the right temperature, pour off all but ¼ cup of water and test again.

Sprinkle the yeast into the warm water and stir with a warmed spoon to dissolve the yeast; set aside.

2. In a large bowl, beat together the eggs, sugar and salt. Stir the yeast mixture again to make sure it is dissolved and then add it and the hot milk to the egg mixture. Stir to blend.

3. Add the flour and beat by hand or with a mixer fitted with dough hooks, to make a smooth batter. Add the butter and beat again.

Pour the dough into the prepared pan and spread it evenly. Cover the pan with a clean dish towel and put it in a draft-free place (for instance, the oven with the heat off) for the batter to rise until almost doubled in volume, about 1½ hours.

4. While the batter is rising, make the rum syrup: Put the sugar and water in a saucepan and bring to a boil, stirring to dissolve the sugar. Boil rapidly, without stirring, until a candy thermometer registers 220°. Remove from the heat, pour in the rum and stir. Set aside for now.

5. When the batter has risen, remove the towel, preheat the oven and bake the cake for 20–25 minutes or until a cake tester inserted in the center of the cake comes out clean. Watch carefully; the cake should be golden brown and no darker.

Let the cake cool in the pan on a wire rack for ten minutes and then cover the pan with an inverted serving platter and turn out the cake rounded side up on the platter.

6. While the cake is still very warm, prick it many times with a fork, all over the inside, outside and top. Pour and spoon the rum syrup *slowly* over the cake, so that the cake absorbs as much syrup as possible. Lift the cake a bit so the puddle of syrup on the platter gets under the cake to soak the bottom, too. Let the cake rest for half an hour.

7. Warm the Apricot Glaze, brush it all over the cake and let the glaze set for one hour.

8. Make the Rum Frosting. Put the frosting in the decorating bag fitted with the star tip (see Decorating Primer, page 27) and pipe four rows of rosettes around the cake: first, on the inside of the ring; second, on the outside of the ring; third and fourth, on the ledges created by the tube pan. For guidance, check the drawing at the beginning of the recipe.

Now pipe trios of rosettes on top of the cake to make flowers, leaving about ½ inch between flowers.

Cut red glacé cherries into small squares and green cherries into wedges; put a red square in the center of each frosting flower and poke one or two green wedges around it, as shown in the drawing.

Refrigerate the cake until half an hour before serving.

RUM FROSTING

MAKES ABOUT 1½ CUPS

½ cup (1 stick) butter, softened
2 cups sifted confectioners' sugar
1 tablespoon light rum

Beat the butter and confectioners' sugar together until smooth. Add the rum and beat again.

GINGERBREAD COTTAGE

MAKES ONE SMALL CAKE, ABOUT 6 × 6 × 6 INCHES

This year, as a change from making the traditional gingerbread cookie house, treat yourself to a maple gingerbread cake cottage with Maple Buttercream Frosting.

BAKING PAN: TWO 8-INCH SQUARE PANS (BROWNIE PANS)
PAN PREPARATION: GREASE AND FLOUR
PREHEAT OVEN TO 350°
BAKING TIME: 30–35 MINUTES

3½ cups flour
2½ teaspoons baking soda
2½ teaspoons ground ginger
1 teaspoon cinnamon
¾ teaspoon salt
1 egg
1 egg yolk
½ cup light brown sugar
1 cup pure maple syrup
1½ cups sour cream
6 tablespoons butter, melted and cooled

Maple Buttercream Frosting (recipe follows on page 157)

For the decoration:
Colored sugar
Thin, rectangular chocolate wafer cookies (usually called Swiss or Neapolitan wafers)
Small round red candies (redhots or imperials)
One jelly fruit slice or other half-round candy
Black or red licorice strings

1. Stir or whisk together the flour, baking soda, spices and salt; set aside.

2. In a large bowl, beat together the whole egg and egg yolk. Gradually add the brown sugar, beating well after each addition. The mixture will be thick and tan-colored.

3. Add the maple syrup, sour cream and melted butter and beat until blended.

4. Add the dry ingredients in four parts, beating well after each addition. Divide the batter equally between the two prepared pans.

5. Bake for 30–35 minutes or until a cake tester inserted in the center of the cake comes out clean. Let the layers cool in the pans on wire racks for ten minutes and then turn them out to finish cooling right side up on the racks.

6. When the layers are completely cool, level the top of each one (how-to, page 24) and then cut each layer into pieces as shown in the drawing.

7. Assemble the cottage: Put the piece labeled *Cottage 1* wrong side up on a flat serving platter or tray. Tuck strips of waxed paper under it to protect the platter (how-to, page 24). Spread ½ cup of Maple Buttercream Frosting on it and cover with the piece labeled *Cottage 2*, wrong side up.

Spread a thin layer of frosting (about ⅓ cup) around the four sides of the cottage and let the frosting set for 30 minutes. Spread another thin layer of frosting (another ⅓–½ cup) over the first layer.

Frost the top of *Cottage 2* with another ½ cup of frosting and place the four roof pieces (*Roof 1–4*) on the frosting; *Roof 1* and *Roof 4* should have their wrong (smooth) sides facing out. Spread a little frosting between the pieces to hold them together as a unit; press them down gently so they are embedded in the frosting. Let the frosting set for 30 minutes.

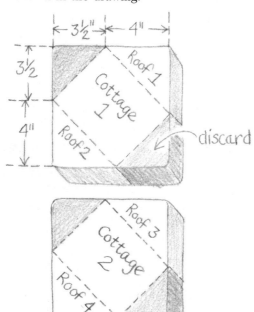

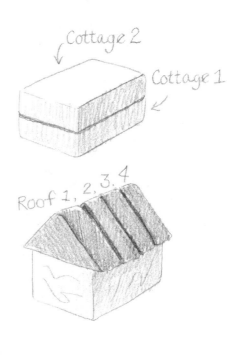

8. Cover the roof (including the flat ends) with frosting, filling in the cracks. Sprinkle colored sugar on the slanted top while the frosting is still tacky; if necessary, roughen the frosting with your fingers or a spatula to restore the tackiness.

9. Decorate the cottage, referring to the drawing at the beginning of the recipe for guidance:

● Press two wafer cookies into one end of the cottage to make the door. Press red candies around the door and a jelly fruit slice above the door.

● Outline the edges of the roof and the sides of the house with red candies.

● Cut pieces of licorice and press them into the sides of the cottage to outline the windows. Cut a wafer cookie into four pieces and press the pieces in place to make the shutters for each pair of windows. Press red candies above and below the windows.

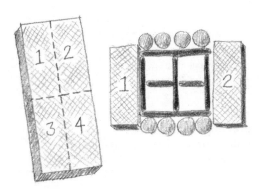

● Cut pieces of licorice and press them into the roof to make the long vertical lines and short horizontal lines.

Gently pull the waxed paper strips away from the cottage. Decorate the serving platter or tray with garlands and small, shiny Christmas balls.

MAPLE BUTTERCREAM FROSTING

MAKES ABOUT 2¾ CUPS

4½ cups confectioners' sugar
Pinch of salt
2½ tablespoons butter, softened
¾ cup maple syrup
1½ tablespoons heavy cream

Sift the confectioners' sugar into a large bowl, add the remaining ingredients and beat until smooth. If necessary, thin with a bit more cream.

YULE LOG

MAKES ONE ROLL ABOUT TEN INCHES LONG

Serve this handsome chocolate sponge roll, filled with Mocha Buttercream Frosting and whipped cream, at your Christmas party or family gathering.

BAKING PAN: ONE 10½ × 15½ × 1-INCH JELLY ROLL PAN
PAN PREPARATION: GREASE, LINE COMPLETELY (BOTTOM AND SIDES) WITH WAXED PAPER; GREASE THE WAXED PAPER
PREHEAT OVEN TO 350°
BAKING TIME: 14–16 MINUTES

½ cup sifted cake flour
¼ cup unsweetened cocoa powder
¼ teaspoon salt
5 eggs, separated
½ cup sugar
1 ounce (1 square) semisweet chocolate, melted and cooled
1 teaspoon vanilla extract
Confectioners' sugar

For the filling and frosting:
2¼ cups Mocha Buttercream Frosting (page 163; double the recipe, using 3½ cups confectioners' sugar)
¾ cup heavy cream, very cold
1 tablespoon sugar

For the decoration:
6 green jelly fruit slices
Small round red candies (redhots or imperials)

1. Stir or whisk together the cake flour, cocoa powder and salt; set aside.

2. In a large bowl, beat the egg yolks until they are thick and pale. Add the sugar one tablespoon at a time, beating well after each addition. When all the sugar is incorporated, beat for two more minutes at high speed.

3. Add the melted chocolate and vanilla and stir gently to blend. Add the dry ingredients in four parts, blending just until moistened. The batter will be stiff.

4. In another large bowl, with clean, dry beaters, beat the egg whites until they stand in firm, glossy, moist peaks. Fold a third of the egg whites into the batter to lighten it; fold the remaining egg whites into the lightened batter. (The folding process will be somewhat difficult because the batter is so stiff.)

Spread the batter evenly in the prepared pan, especially into the corners, and put it in the oven immediately.

5. Bake for 14–16 minutes or until a cake tester inserted in the center of the cake comes out clean. Do not overbake.

While the cake is baking, get out a clean linen or other lint-free dish towel and a wire rack or cookie sheet larger than the jelly roll pan.

When the cake is done, take the pan out of the oven. Working quickly, cover the pan first with the dish towel and then with the inverted wire rack or cookie sheet. Flip the pan, towel and rack or cookie sheet to turn out the cake. Remove the pan and then slowly and carefully peel off the waxed paper.

Slide the towel and cake onto the table or counter; the cake is wrong side up. Cut off any crisp edges of the cake and sift a little confectioners' sugar over it. Fold one end of the towel over the short end of the cake and roll the cake up in the towel. Place the rolled cake seam side down on the wire rack to cool.

6. Unroll the cooled cake and spread 1¼ cups of Mocha Buttercream Frosting evenly on it.

Whip the heavy cream, mixed with the tablespoon of sugar, until stiff. Spread a layer of whipped cream on the frosting, making the layer thinner at the end of the cake that was rolled first.

Roll up the cake and filling, this time without the towel (but using the towel to help roll), and place the roll seam side down on a serving platter. Refrigerate the cake for an hour to firm the filling.

7. Take the filled cake roll out of the refrigerator and trim a thin slice from one end and a ½-inch-thick slice from the other end. Discard (or taste-test) the thin slice and reserve the ½-inch-thick slice.

Spread a little buttercream on the top center of the cake and press the reserved slice on it to make the "knothole."

Now frost the entire cake with the remaining frosting, building the frosting up around the sides of the knothole (do *not*

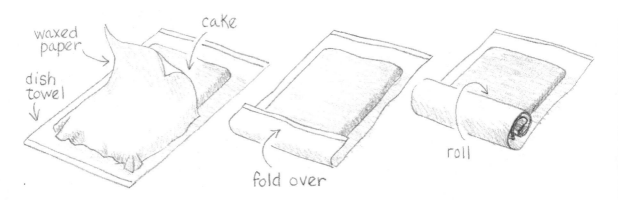

cover the top of the knothole) and working the frosting as far under the roll as you can. Draw a metal spatula lengthwise through the frosting to simulate the rough texture of bark.

8. Make the decorations: Following the pattern below, cut each green jelly fruit slice into a holly leaf. Arrange the six leaves and a few red candies on the cake as shown in the drawing at the beginning of the recipe, pressing the candy firmly into the frosting.

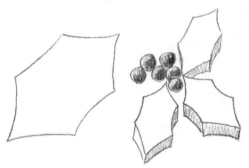

CAKES TO MAKE FOR HOLIDAY GIFTS:

Chocolate Pound Cake, page 49
Rum Raisin Pound Cake, page 62
Apricot-Orange or Currant-Orange Tea Loaves, page 66
Dark Sweet Date-Nut Loaf, page 67
Pecan Spice Loaves, page 68
Filled Vienna Braid, page 74
Filled Ring, page 75
Southern Bourbon Pecan Cake, page 102

CHAPTER 11

Frostings, Fillings and Glazes

BASIC VANILLA BUTTERCREAM FROSTING

FLAVORED BUTTERCREAM FROSTING

MOCHA OR CHOCOLATE BUTTERCREAM FROSTING

LEMON OR ORANGE BUTTERCREAM FROSTING

COCONUT PECAN CARAMEL FROSTING

SNOWDRIFT FROSTING

DOUBLE CHOCOLATE FROSTING

CREAMY CHOCOLATE FROSTING

BASIC SWEETENED WHIPPED CREAM

FLAVORED WHIPPED CREAM

SOUR CREAM FROSTING

CREAM CHEESE FROSTING

BASIC VANILLA PASTRY CREAM

FLAVORED PASTRY CREAM

VANILLA GLAZE

SEMISWEET CHOCOLATE GLAZE

EASY BITTERSWEET CHOCOLATE GLAZE

MOCHA GLAZE

RUM OR BRANDY GLAZE

APRICOT GLAZE

BASIC VANILLA BUTTERCREAM FROSTING

This versatile uncooked vanilla buttercream can be used as the basis for several smooth and chunky variations. Note that it is made with superfine sugar as well as confectioners' sugar, in order to lessen the cornstarch taste so often present in buttercreams made only with confectioners' sugar.

Ingredients are given for three different amounts of frosting, so you can make just as much as you need. The instructions are the same for all three amounts.

To make 1½ cups:
½ cup superfine sugar
1 egg yolk
Pinch of salt
1½ teaspoons vanilla extract
2½ tablespoons heavy cream
¼ cup (½ stick) butter, softened
2 cups sifted confectioners' sugar

To make 3 cups:
1 cup superfine sugar
2 egg yolks
Pinch of salt
1 tablespoon vanilla extract
¼ cup heavy cream
½ cup (1 stick) butter, softened
3½ cups sifted confectioners' sugar

To make 6 cups:
2 cups superfine sugar
4 egg yolks
¼ teaspoon salt
2 tablespoons vanilla extract
½ cup heavy cream
1 cup (2 sticks) butter, softened
7–7½ cups sifted confectioners' sugar

1. In a large bowl, combine the superfine sugar, egg yolk(s), salt, vanilla and heavy cream and beat for eight minutes at medium speed.

2. In another large bowl, without washing the beaters, cream the butter until light. Add the yolk mixture a little at a time, beating well after each addition. When you are finished beating, the superfine sugar should be almost completely dissolved.

3. Gradually add the confectioners' sugar, beating well after each addition. The finished buttercream should be smooth and spreadable. If necessary, add a little more cream to thin it and beat again. If the buttercream seems too thin, add a little more confectioners' sugar and a bit of butter and beat again.

FLAVORED BUTTERCREAM FROSTING

These variations are made by adding flavoring or chunky ingredients to prepared Basic Vanilla Buttercream Frosting.

EASY CHOCOLATE BUTTER-CREAM FROSTING: For each cup of Basic Vanilla Buttercream Frosting, add two tablespoons of unsweetened cocoa powder and one tablespoon of heavy cream; beat until smooth.

PINEAPPLE-COCONUT CHUNKY BUTTERCREAM FROSTING: Drain, pat dry on paper towels and chop ¾ cup of pineapple chunks for each cup of Basic Vanilla Buttercream Frosting. Add the chopped pineapple and one cup of flaked, unsweetened coconut to the frosting and stir well. Yields two cups of chunky frosting for each cup of vanilla buttercream.

NOTE: Refrigerate the frosted cake until serving time, to keep the frosting firm.

CHOCOLATE-NUT CHUNKY BUTTERCREAM FROSTING: For each 1½ cups of Basic Vanilla Buttercream Frosting, stir in ½ cup of chopped, toasted almonds or pecans, ½ cup of chopped white or semisweet chocolate and one tablespoon of milk or cream. Yields two cups of chunky frosting for each 1½ cups of vanilla buttercream.

COFFEE BUTTERCREAM FROSTING: For each cup of Basic Vanilla Buttercream Frosting, add 1½ teaspoons of powdered instant coffee dissolved in one tablespoon of hot cream, and one tablespoon of confectioners' sugar; beat until smooth.

NOTE: To make powdered instant coffee, put a few teaspoons of instant coffee granules in a plastic bag and crush them with a rolling pin. Measure out the powdered coffee as needed.

MOCHA OR CHOCOLATE BUTTERCREAM FROSTING

MAKES ABOUT 1½ CUPS

To use Mocha or Chocolate Buttercream Frosting for both frosting and filling, double the recipe to make about 3½ cups of frosting. This buttercream is excellent for piping, too.

3 tablespoons heavy cream
2 ounces (2 squares) semisweet chocolate
2 teaspoons instant coffee granules *or* 2 teaspoons unsweetened cocoa powder

¼ cup (½ stick) butter, softened
½ cup superfine sugar
1 egg yolk
Pinch of salt
1½ teaspoons vanilla extract
1¾–2 cups sifted confectioners' sugar

1. Heat the cream and chocolate in a small saucepan over low heat, stirring to melt and blend. *If you are making mocha buttercream,* add the instant coffee and stir to dissolve the coffee. Set aside to cool.

2. Cream the butter until light. Add the superfine sugar one tablespoon at a time, beating well after each addition. *If you are making chocolate buttercream,* add the cocoa powder and beat again.

3. Add the melted chocolate mixture, egg yolk, salt and vanilla and beat until the superfine sugar is dissolved.

4. Add the confectioners' sugar ¼ cup at a time, beating well after each addition. A total of 1¾ cups of confectioners' sugar (3½ cups if you have doubled the recipe) makes a good spreading consistency; if necessary, add more cream a few drops at a time to thin the frosting. A total of two cups of confectioners' sugar (four cups if you have doubled the recipe) makes the frosting just right for piping.

LEMON OR ORANGE BUTTERCREAM FROSTING

MAKES ABOUT THREE CUPS

This kind of buttercream is called a "cooked" buttercream because it is made with boiled sugar syrup instead of confectioners' sugar. To make it, you will need a candy thermometer for measuring the temperature of the boiling syrup.

¼ cup fresh lemon juice *or* ¼ cup
    pure orange juice
¼ cup water
¾ cup sugar
1½ teaspoons light corn syrup
6 egg yolks

1 heaping teaspoon grated lemon
    rind *or* 3 heaping teaspoons
    grated orange rind
½ teaspoon vanilla extract
1½ cups (3 sticks) butter, softened

1. In a heavy saucepan, stir the lemon (or orange) juice, water, sugar and corn syrup over medium heat until the mixture comes to a boil and the sugar is completely dissolved.

Let the syrup boil gently, without stirring, until it reaches 240° (soft ball stage) on a candy thermometer. Remove from the heat and allow to cool slightly while you complete step 2.

2. In a large bowl, beat the egg yolks until they are pale and thick and fall in a ribbon when you lift the beaters.

3. Add the hot syrup to the egg yolks by pouring the syrup down the side of the bowl a little at a time, beating well after each addition. (Pouring down the side of the bowl prevents the stream of syrup from touching the beaters and forming a spun-sugar thread.)

Add the grated rind and the vanilla and beat again.

4. Add the butter one tablespoon at a time, beating well after each addition. The frosting is done when all the butter is incorporated and the mixture is thick and perfectly smooth.

It's best to use this buttercream as soon as possible, but you may refrigerate it for a few days if necessary. When you take it out of the refrigerator, let it come to room temperature and then beat until it is smooth and spreadable again.

COCONUT PECAN CARAMEL FROSTING

MAKES ABOUT THREE CUPS

Crunchy, chewy and delicious—an unusual buttercream made with caramel syrup and a little molasses instead of the brown sugar generally used in caramel frostings.

For the caramel syrup:
⅓ cup sugar
⅓ cup boiling water

10 tablespoons butter, softened
2½ cups sifted confectioners' sugar
2 teaspoons unsulphured molasses

1 egg yolk
1 tablespoon heavy cream
½ teaspoon vanilla extract
1 cup toasted, shredded (or flaked)
    unsweetened coconut (how-to,
    pages 15–16)
1 cup chopped pecans

1. Make the caramel syrup: Put the ⅓ cup of sugar into an 8-inch skillet over medium heat. Cook, stirring, until the sugar melts and turns first golden and then a darker amber. This will happen just as the sugar begins to boil. Remove the skillet from the heat.

Very carefully, add the boiling water *one tablespoonful at a time*, stirring constantly with a long-handled spoon; the hot syrup will bubble and spatter, so stand back from the pan. Return the skillet to low heat and cook the syrup for a few minutes, stirring constantly, until all the lumps and stickiness have dissolved.

Pour the syrup into a measuring cup and set aside to cool; you should have a little more than ⅓ cup of syrup.

2. In a large bowl, beat the butter until light. Add one cup of the confectioners' sugar and beat until smooth.

3. Add the molasses, egg yolk, cream and vanilla and beat well. Add the caramel syrup a little at a time, beating well after each addition.

4. Gradually beat in the remaining 1½ cups of confectioners' sugar.

5. Stir in the toasted coconut and the chopped pecans.

SNOWDRIFT FROSTING

MAKES ABOUT 2½ CUPS OR 4½ CUPS

This frosting is a cross between traditional White Mountain Frosting and a good buttercream: It has the fluffiness of an egg-white-and-sugar-syrup frosting and the delicious taste of frosting made with butter.

TIP: Snowdrift Frosting should be spread on generously when you are filling and frosting a cake. The recipe for the smaller amount yields enough to fill and frost a two-layer cake and the larger amount is more than enough to fill and frost a three-layer cake. Use Snowdrift Frosting as soon as possible after you make it. The frosting will separate if it is chilled, so it should *not* be stored in the refrigerator for later use; cakes frosted with Snowdrift Frosting should be stored in a cake preserver, not in the refrigerator or freezer.

For 2½ cups:
½ cup water
4 teaspoons light corn syrup
1 cup sugar
3 egg whites
1 cup (2 sticks) butter, softened
1 teaspoon vanilla extract
Pinch of salt

For 4½ cups:
¾ cup water
2 tablespoons light corn syrup
1½ cups sugar
5 egg whites
1½ cups (3 sticks) butter, softened
2 teaspoons vanilla extract
Pinch of salt

1. Put the water, corn syrup and ⅔ cup of the sugar (one cup of the sugar for the larger amount of frosting) in a heavy saucepan over low heat and stir until the sugar is dissolved. Raise the heat to medium and bring to a boil. Boil without stirring until the temperature registers 240° (soft ball stage) on a candy thermometer. Turn off the heat.

2. In a large bowl, beat the egg whites until foamy. Gradually add the remaining sugar while beating the egg whites continuously. Beat until the egg whites hold firm, glossy, moist peaks.

3. Slowly pour the hot syrup down the side of the bowl into the egg whites (so the syrup does not come into direct contact with the beaters), beating continuously. Beat until the mixture is smooth and stiff, like thick marshmallow cream; set aside.

4. In another large bowl, without washing the beaters, cream the butter until light. Add the egg white mixture to the butter about one sixth at a time, beating well after each addition. Add the vanilla and salt and blend until smooth.

DOUBLE CHOCOLATE FROSTING

MAKES ABOUT THREE CUPS

½ cup butter, softened
2 eggs
2 teaspoons vanilla extract
¼ teaspoon salt

4 ounces (4 squares) semisweet
    chocolate, melted and cooled
½ cup unsweetened cocoa powder
3 cups sifted confectioners' sugar

1. In a large bowl, cream the butter until light. Add the eggs, vanilla, salt and melted chocolate and beat well.
2. Sift the cocoa powder into the butter mixture and beat again. Add the confectioners' sugar, ½ cup at a time, beating well after each addition.

The frosting should be a perfect spreading consistency, but if necessary you may thin it by beating in a little milk or cream.

CREAMY CHOCOLATE FROSTING

MAKES ABOUT 3½ CUPS

A light, airy chocolate frosting with a mild chocolate flavor.

3 tablespoons unsweetened cocoa
    powder
¼ cup flour
⅔ cup water

1 egg
⅔ cup sugar
1½ cups heavy cream, very cold

1. Stir together the cocoa powder and flour. Gradually add the water, stirring until smooth.
2. In another bowl, beat the egg and sugar together until the mixture is thick and pale. Pour the egg mixture and the cocoa mixture into a heavy saucepan and stir to blend.
3. Cook over low heat, stirring constantly, until smooth and very thick. Be patient; this may take about 20 minutes. Remove the saucepan from the heat and let the mixture cool completely, stirring occasionally to release more heat.
4. When the chocolate mixture is cool, whip the cream until stiff. Fold about a third of the whipped cream into the chocolate mixture to lighten it; fold the rest of the whipped cream into the lightened mixture.

BASIC SWEETENED WHIPPED CREAM

MAKES ABOUT TWO CUPS

Heavy cream approximately doubles in volume when you whip it. Therefore, decide how much *whipped* cream you want to end up with and divide that amount in half—that's how much *liquid* heavy cream you must have on hand. For example, if you need three cups of *whipped* cream, begin with 1½ cups of *liquid* cream.

Basic and flavored whipped creams are excellent for piping (how-to, pages 27–29).

TIP: Whipped cream may be stored in the refrigerator for several hours, but eventually it begins to deflate. It's best to whip the cream just before you need it.

1 cup heavy cream, very cold
2 tablespoons confectioners' sugar

Put the cream and sugar in a deep bowl; beat at low speed until the cream is stiff. Do not overbeat or the cream may turn to butter.

NOTE: Beating the cream at low speed takes longer than beating it at high speed, but the whipped cream will have more volume and you'll have better control while you whip.

FLAVORED WHIPPED CREAM

To make about two cups of flavored whipped cream, put one cup of heavy cream in a deep bowl with the additional ingredients listed in any one entry below; beat at low speed until the cream is stiff.

VANILLA WHIPPED CREAM: Two to three tablespoons confectioners' sugar and two teaspoons vanilla extract

CHOCOLATE WHIPPED CREAM: Three tablespoons confectioners' sugar, ½ teaspoon vanilla extract and two tablespoons sifted unsweetened cocoa powder

COFFEE WHIPPED CREAM: Four tablespoons confectioners' sugar and 1½ teaspoons powdered instant coffee

NOTE: To turn instant coffee granules into powder, put a few teaspoons of granules in a plastic bag and crush them with a rolling pin. Measure out the powdered coffee as needed.

SOUR CREAM FROSTING

MAKES ABOUT THREE CUPS

Many sour cream frostings are just thin toppings. This one is different—
it's fluffy and rich enough to be used as a filling as well as a frosting.

1 tablespoon cornstarch
5 tablespoons sugar
2 egg yolks

1 cup sour cream
1 cup heavy cream, very cold
1 teaspoon vanilla extract

1. Stir together the cornstarch and four tablespoons of the sugar.

2. Put the egg yolks in the top pan of a double boiler and add the cornstarch mixture. Whisk together until smooth. Add the sour cream and blend well.

3. Fill the bottom pan of the double boiler about one-third full of water and bring the water to an active simmer. Cook the sour cream mixture over the simmering water for several minutes until thickened; if the mixture becomes lumpy, stir it briskly with a whisk. Remove the top pan and let the mixture cool completely.

4. Whip the heavy cream with the remaining tablespoon of sugar and the vanilla until the cream is stiff. Fold the cooled sour cream mixture into the whipped cream.

Refrigerate until needed.

CREAM CHEESE FROSTING

MAKES ABOUT TWO CUPS

½ pound (one 8-ounce package)
cream cheese, softened
2 tablespoons butter, softened

2 cups sifted confectioners' sugar
1 teaspoon vanilla extract
1 teaspoon grated lemon rind

Beat together the cream cheese and butter until light and smooth. Gradually add the confectioners' sugar, beating well after each addition. Add the vanilla and lemon rind and beat until blended.

CHOCOLATE CREAM CHEESE FROSTING: Make Cream Cheese Frosting, omitting the lemon rind if desired. Add two ounces (two squares) of melted, cooled unsweetened chocolate and two additional tablespoons of confectioners' sugar. Blend until smooth.

BASIC VANILLA PASTRY CREAM

MAKES 1¼ CUPS OR 2½ CUPS

For 1¼ cups:
1 cup milk
3 egg yolks
⅓ cup sugar
2 tablespoons flour

Pinch of salt
1 tablespoon butter, softened
1 teaspoon vanilla extract

For 2½ cups:
Double the ingredients listed above

1. Scald the milk in a medium-size, heavy saucepan. Turn off the heat and cover the pan.

2. In a large bowl, beat the egg yolks and sugar until the mixture is pale and forms a ribbon when you lift the beaters.

3. Use a fine strainer to sift the flour and salt over the egg mixture; blend thoroughly. Add ½ cup of the hot milk to the egg mixture, stirring well to warm the egg mixture. Now add all the egg mixture to the hot milk in the saucepan. Bring to a boil over medium heat, stirring constantly. (Be sure to get your spoon into the curve of the saucepan.) The mixture will be lumpy.

Immediately reduce the heat to very low and continue cooking for another minute, stirring constantly, until the mixture thickens and becomes smooth. Remove from the heat and continue stirring for three more minutes to release more heat.

4. Add the butter and vanilla and stir for another minute or two, until the butter is melted and incorporated.

If you are going to add additional ingredients to make a flavored pastry cream, allow the Basic Vanilla Pastry Cream to cool until it is just warm and then follow the instructions given on page 171 for the flavor you choose.

Cover the finished pastry cream with a piece of plastic wrap, pressing the wrap directly onto the surface of the pastry cream to cover it completely; this prevents a skin from forming.

Let the pastry cream cool and then refrigerate until needed.

FLAVORED PASTRY CREAM

MAKES ABOUT 1½ CUPS OR THREE CUPS

To make flavored pastry cream, combine the flavoring ingredients (listed below) with the indicated amount of *warm* Basic Vanilla Pastry Cream (page 170) and blend until smooth.

ALMOND PASTRY CREAM: To make 1½ cups, combine 1¼ cups of warm Basic Vanilla Pastry Cream (page 170) with ½ cup of ground almonds (either toasted or raw), one tablespoon of softened butter and ¼ teaspoon of almond extract. Stir the ingredients vigorously until the butter is melted and incorporated.

Double the ingredients to make three cups of Almond Pastry Cream.

CHOCOLATE PASTRY CREAM: To make 1½ cups, melt one ounce (one square) of semisweet chocolate and one ounce of unsweetened chocolate in a small saucepan; let the chocolate cool. Gradually add the melted chocolate to 1¼ cups of warm Basic Vanilla Pastry Cream (page 170), stirring until thoroughly blended.

Double the ingredients to make three cups of Chocolate Pastry Cream.

COFFEE PASTRY CREAM: To make 1¼ cups, add two teaspoons of powdered instant coffee to 1¼ cups of warm Basic Vanilla Pastry Cream (page 170) and stir until thoroughly blended.

Double the ingredients to make 2½ cups of Coffee Pastry Cream.

NOTE: To make powdered instant coffee, put several teaspoons of instant coffee granules in a plastic bag and crush them with a rolling pin. Measure the powdered coffee as needed.

LEMON PASTRY CREAM: To make 1¼ cups, combine 1¼ cups of warm Basic Vanilla Pastry Cream (page 170) with one teaspoon of grated lemon rind and one tablespoon of fresh lemon juice and stir until thoroughly blended.

Double the ingredients to make 2½ cups of Lemon Pastry Cream.

VANILLA GLAZE

MAKES ABOUT ⅔ CUP

1 tablespoon butter, melted
1 teaspoon vanilla
2½ tablespoons milk
Pinch of salt
2 cups sifted confectioners' sugar

Stir together the butter, vanilla, milk and salt. Add the confectioners' sugar and beat until smooth. If the glaze is too thin, beat in a bit more sifted confectioners' sugar; if it is too thick, add a little more milk or cream.

This glaze sets and dries quickly; to prevent a crust from forming, cover the unused portion with a piece of plastic wrap pressed directly onto the surface of the glaze.

SEMISWEET CHOCOLATE GLAZE

MAKES ABOUT 1½ CUPS

A versatile glaze that may be halved or doubled with complete success.

2 ounces (2 squares) unsweetened
  chocolate
¼ cup (½ stick) butter
6 tablespoons heavy cream
1 teaspoon vanilla extract
2 cups sifted confectioners' sugar

1. Fill the bottom pan of a double boiler half full of water and bring it to a simmer. Fit the top pan over the simmering water. Put the chocolate and butter in the top pan and stir until melted and smooth. Turn off the heat.

2. Leaving the pan over the hot water, add the remaining ingredients and beat with a wire whisk until smooth.

The glaze will thicken as it cools, so leave it over the hot water until needed.

EASY BITTERSWEET CHOCOLATE GLAZE

MAKES ABOUT ONE CUP

A thin, shiny glaze perfect for pouring over tortes and other cakes that must be coated completely. It takes several hours to set, allowing plenty of time for adding decorations like chopped nuts or chocolate curls. If you prefer a slightly sweeter glaze, use all semisweet chocolate instead of the combination of unsweetened and semisweet chocolates.

TIP: The glaze hardens and changes from a shiny to a dull finish when it is refrigerated.

3 ounces (3 squares) unsweetened
  chocolate
6 ounces (6 squares) semisweet
  chocolate
4 teaspoons vegetable oil

Put the chocolate and the oil in a heavy saucepan and melt over very low heat, stirring until smooth. Transfer to a small pitcher or measuring cup for easy pouring.

MOCHA GLAZE

MAKES ABOUT ONE CUP

2 ounces (2 squares) unsweetened
   chocolate
2 tablespoons butter
¼ cup strong coffee
½ teaspoon vanilla extract
1⅓ cups sifted confectioners' sugar

Put the chocolate, butter and coffee in
a small saucepan over low heat and stir
until blended. Add the vanilla and stir
again. Transfer the mixture to a bowl, add
the confectioners' sugar and beat until
smooth.

If necessary, thin with a little more
coffee or thicken with a little more confectioners' sugar.

RUM OR BRANDY GLAZE

MAKES ABOUT ONE CUP

2½ cups sifted confectioners' sugar
¼ cup light rum or brandy
1 teaspoon vanilla extract
1 tablespoon butter, very soft

Put all the ingredients in a bowl and
beat until smooth. If necessary, thin with a
little more rum or brandy or thicken with
a little more sifted confectioners' sugar.

APRICOT GLAZE

MAKES ABOUT ONE CUP

One 12-ounce or 18-ounce jar of
   apricot jam
2 tablespoons orange juice, orange
   liqueur or water

1. Put the jam in a small saucepan over
low heat and stir until melted and very
hot. Do not boil.
2. Place a fine strainer over a bowl.
Pour the hot jam into the strainer a little at
a time, pressing it through the wire mesh
with a spoon. The liquid jam in the bowl
will be used to make the glaze. (If you
wish, save the pieces of apricot left in the
strainer; they may be re-mixed with any
leftover glaze to make a thick jam.)
3. Return the liquid jam to the saucepan. Add the orange juice, liqueur or water
and stir well. The glaze should be quite
runny, about the consistency of thick tomato
juice. Add one more tablespoon of juice,
liqueur or water if necessary.

Warm the glaze occasionally while
you are using it because it thickens as it
cools.

OTHER FROSTINGS, FILLINGS AND GLAZES TO MAKE:

Chestnut Filling, page 60
Prune Filling, page 76
Tart Lemon Glaze, page 76
Almond Filling, page 77
Butterscotch Glaze, page 77
Apricot Filling, page 77

Cream Glaze, page 77
Homemade Applesauce, page 107
Honey Glaze, page 148
Hard Sauce, page 152
Rum Frosting, page 154
Maple Buttercream Frosting, page 157

Index

Almond Paste Fruits, 149
Almond Pound Cake, 62–63
Almond Tea Cakes, 65
almonds, 51, 52, 62–63, 65, 77, 171
apple cakes, 93–94, 106–107
applesauce, 107
Applesauce Stack Cake, 106–107
Apricot-Orange Tea Loaves, 66
apricots, 66, 77, 173

baking information, 12, 20–21
Banana Layer Cake, 99
Bear Claws, 72–73, 76
birthday cakes and decorations, 111–124
    cupcakes, 122–124
    ice cream cakes, 118–119, 120–121
    layer cakes, 113–114, 118–119
    sheet cakes, 115–117
blueberries, 83–84, 89
brownie cake, 48–49
butter sponge cakes
    Butter Sponge Layer Cake, 34–35
    Butter Sponge Torte with Pecans and Coffee
        Crunch Filling, 130–131
    Miniature Iced Cakes, 134–135
    Raspberries-and-Cream Cake, 88
buttercream frostings, 157, 162–165
buttermilk, 64, 89
Butterscotch Glaze, 77

cake-making, 11–30
caramel frosting, with coconut and pecans, 165
Caramelized Apple Cake, 93–94
Caramelized Pecans, 131
carrot cake, 69
cheesecakes, 56–57, 104–105, 136–137
Chestnut Filling, 60
chocolate cakes, 47–60
    Chocolate Almond Sand Cake, 52
    Chocolate Brownie Cake, 48–49
    Chocolate Cheesecake with Cherry Topping,
        56–57
    Chocolate Grand Marnier Torte, 140–141
    Chocolate Layer Cake, 40–41
    Chocolate Pound Cake, 49
    Light Chocolate Cake, 50–51
    Mississippi Mud Cake, 98
    Mocha Sponge Roll, 58–59
    South American Chocolate Cake, 53

    Strawberry-Crowned Devil's Food Cake, 54–55
    Yule Log, 158–160
chocolate frostings, fillings and glazes, 121, 163–164,
    167, 168, 169, 171, 172
chocolate, general information, 15
Christmas cakes, 143–160
    Christmas Rum Ring, 153–154
    Christmas Tree Cake, 145–146
    Figgy Fruitcake with Hard Sauce, 152
    Gingerbread Cottage, 155–157
    Glazed Nut Cake with Almond Paste Fruits,
        147–149
    Holiday Jam Cake with Sugarplums, 144
    Whiskey Fruitcake, 150–151
    Yule Log, 158–160
Cinnamon Prune Yogurt Cake, 82
coconut layer cake, 108–109
coffee frostings, fillings and glazes, 163, 168, 171
coffeecakes, 71–84
coffeecakes, quick
    Cinnamon Prune Yogurt Cake, 82
    Peach and Blueberry Kuchen, 83–84
    Quick Rich Little Coffeecakes, 78
    Raisin Bran Batter Cake, 79
coffeecakes, yeast
    basic yeast dough for, 72–73
    Bear Claws, 76
    Filled Ring, 75
    Filled Vienna Braid, 74
    fillings and glazes for, 76–77
    Folded Pockets, 75
    Honey Pecan Pull-Aparts, 80–81
Covering Icing, 135
Cranberry-Filled Lemon Loaf, 90
Cream Cheese Frosting, 169
Cream Glaze, 77
cupcakes, fancy, 122–124
Currant-Orange Tea Loaves, 66

date-nut loaf, 67
Decorating Frosting, 30
Decorating Primer, 25–30
devil's food cake, with strawberries, 54–55

Easter Cake, 33
equipment for making cakes, 13–14
extravagant cakes, 125–142
    Butter Sponge Torte with Pecans and Coffee
        Crunch Filling, 130–131

Celebration Cake, 132–133
Chocolate Grand Marnier Torte, 140–141
Fresh Coconut Layer Cake, 108–109
Glazed Nut Cake with Almond Paste Fruits,
    147–149
Hazelnut Cheesecake, 136–137
Miniature Iced Cakes, 134–135
Mocha Sponge Roll, 58–60
Raspberries-and-Cream Cake, 88
Two-Tiered Heart Cake, 126–129
Vanilla Meringue Cake, 138–139

Father's Day Cake, 41
Figgy Fruitcake with Hard Sauce, 152
Filled Ring, 72–73, 75
Filled Vienna Braid, 72–73, 74
filling, frosting and glazing, general information,
    23–24
frostings, fillings and glazes, 161–173
    almond, 77, 171
    applesauce, 107
    apricot, 77, 173
    buttercream frosting, 157, 162–165
    Butterscotch Glaze, 77
    Chestnut Filling, 60
    chocolate, 121, 163–164, 167, 168, 169, 171, 172,
        179
    chunky frostings, 163
    Coconut Pecan Caramel Frosting, 165
    Covering Icing, 135
    Cream Cheese Frosting, 169
    Cream Glaze, 77
    Decorating Frosting (for piping), 30
    general information about, 23–24
    Hard Sauce, 152
    Honey Glaze, 148
    lemon, 76, 164–165, 171
    Maple Buttercream Frosting, 157
    mocha, 163–164, 173
    pastry cream, 170–171
    Pineapple-Coconut Chunky Buttercream Frost-
        ing, 163
    Prune Filling, 76
    rum or brandy, 154, 173
    Snowdrift Frosting, 166
    Sour Cream Frosting, 169
    vanilla, 162, 168, 170, 172
    whipped cream, basic and flavored, 168
fruit, dried or canned, in cakes
    apricots, 66, 77
    cherries, 56, 57
    currants, 66

dates, 67
figs, 152
mixed dried fruits, 150–151
pineapple, 103, 163
prunes, 76, 82, 144
raisins, 62–63, 79
fruit, fresh, cakes with, 85–96
    Applesauce Stack Cake, 106–107
    Banana Layer Cake, 99
    Blueberry Buttermilk Spice Squares, 89
    Caramelized Apple Cake, 93–94
    Cranberry-Filled Lemon Loaf, 90
    Peach and Blueberry Kuchen, 83–84
    Quick Plum Cake, 95–96
    Raspberries-and-Cream Cake, 88
    Strawberry-Crowned Devil's Food Cake, 54–55
    Strawberry Shortcake, 86–87
    Walnut Ginger Pear Torte, 91–92
fruitcake, 150–151, 152

genoise (butter sponge cakes), 34–35, 88, 130–131,
    134–135
Gingerbread Cottage, 155–157
glazes, 76, 77, 148, 172–173

Halloween Cake, 45
Hard Sauce, 152
Hazelnut Cheesecake, 136–137
Holiday Jam Cake with Sugarplums, 144
Honey Glaze, 148
Honey Pecan Pull-Aparts, 80–81

ice cream cakes, 118–119, 120–121
ingredients, general information, 12–13, 15–17

jam cake, 144
jam roll, 100

layer cakes and decorations, 31–45
    Banana Layer Cake, 99
    Birthday Layer Cakes, 113–114
    Burnt Sugar Layer Cake, 44–45
    Butter Sponge Layer Cake, 34–35
    Celebration Cake, 132–133
    Chocolate Layer Cake, 40–41
    Fresh Coconut Layer Cake, 108–109
    Ice Cream Layer Cake, 118–119
    Lemon Layer Cake, 42–43
    Light Chocolate Cake, 50–51
    marble, 38–39
    Raspberries-and-Cream Cake, 88
    spice, 144, 155–157

Sweet Cream Layer Cake, 38–39
Sweet Cream Marble Cake, 38–39
White Layer Cake, 36–37
Yellow Layer Cake, 32–33
lemon cakes, 42–43, 64, 90, 132–133
lemon frostings, fillings and glazes, 76, 164–165, 171

macaroons, crisp almond, 51
making cakes, 11–30
Maple Buttercream Frosting, 157
marble cakes, 38–39, 62–63
Marble Pound Cake, 62–63
meringue cake and meringue kisses, 138–139
Miniature Iced Cakes, 134–135
Mississippi Mud Cake, 98
mocha frostings, 163–164, 173
Mocha Sponge Roll, 58–59
Mother's Day Cake, 39

New York Cheesecake, 104–105
nut fillings, 60, 77
nuts, cakes with
    almonds, 50–51, 52, 62–63, 65
    Glazed Nut Cake with Almond Paste Fruits,
        147–149
    Hazelnut Cheesecake, 136–137
    pecans, 68, 80–81, 102, 130–131
    walnuts, 67, 91–92, 99
nuts, general information, 16–17

pastry cream, 170–171
Peach and Blueberry Kuchen, 83–84
pear torte, 91–92
pecan cakes, 67, 80–81, 102, 130–131
pecan, coconut caramel frosting, 165
Pecan Spice Loaves, 68
pecans, caramelized, 131
Pineapple-Coconut Chunky Buttercream Frosting, 163
Pineapple Upside-Down Cake, 103
piping, general information, 27–29
plum cake, 95–96
pound cakes, tea loaves and snack cakes, 61–70
    Almond Pound Cake, 62–63
    Almond Tea Cakes, 65
    Apricot-Orange or Currant-Orange Tea Loaves,
        66
    Best Carrot Cake Squares, 69
    Blueberry Buttermilk Spice Squares, 89
    Buttermilk Lemon Pound Cake, 64
    Chocolate Pound Cake, 49
    Cranberry-Filled Lemon Loaf, 90
    Dark Sweet Date-Nut Loaf, 67
    Marble Pound Cake, 62–63

Pecan Spice Loaves, 68
Perfect Pound Cake and Variations, 62–63
Pineapple Upside-Down Cake, 103
Rum Raisin Pound Cake, 62–63
prunes, 76, 82

Raisin Bran Batter Cake, 79
raisins, 62–63, 79
Raspberries-and-Cream Cake, 88
Rich Chocolate Sauce, 121
rolled cakes, 58–59, 100, 120, 158–160
rum, Christmas ring, 153
Rum Frosting, 154
Rum Raisin Pound Cake, 62–63

Snowdrift Frosting, 166
Sour Cream Frosting, 169
South American Chocolate Cake, 53
Southern Bourbon Pecan Cake, 102
spice cakes, 68, 82, 89, 91–92, 144, 155–157
storing cakes, 22–23
strawberries, chocolate-dipped, 54
Strawberry Shortcake, 86–87

techniques, basic, 18–20
Thanksgiving Cake, 37
traditional cakes, 97–109
    Applesauce Stack Cake, 106–107
    Banana Layer Cake, 99
    Burnt Sugar Layer Cake, 44–45
    Dark Sweet Date-Nut Loaf, 67
    Filled Vienna Braid, 72–73, 74
    Fresh Coconut Layer Cake, 108–109
    Honey Pecan Pull-Aparts, 80–81
    Mississippi Mud Cake, 98
    New York Cheesecake, 104–105
    Old-Fashioned Jam Roll, 100–101
    Pineapple Upside-Down Cake, 103
    Southern Bourbon Pecan Cake, 102
    Strawberry Shortcake, 86–87

upside-down cakes, 93–94, 103

vanilla frostings, fillings and glazes, 162, 168, 170, 172
Vanilla Meringue Cake, 138–139

Walnut Ginger Pear Torte, 91–92
wedding cake, 125, 126–129
whipped cream, basic and flavored, 168
Whiskey Fruitcake, 150–151

yeast dough, basic, 72–73
Yule Log, 158–160